BASS PLAYER PRESENTS

THE FRETLESS BASS

BASS PLAYER
PRESENTS

THE FRETLESS BASS

·········· 𝄢 ··········

EDITED BY CHRIS JISI

Backbeat Books

An Imprint of Hal Leonard Corporation
New York

Published in 2008 by Backbeat Books
An Imprint of Hal Leonard Corporation
7777 West Bluemound Road
Milwaukee, WI 53213

Trade Book Division Editorial Offices
19 West 21st Street, New York, NY 10010

Printed in the United States of America

Book design by Damien Castaneda

Photo credits:
Page 2: Jill Furmanovsky; courtesy of Jack Bruce. Page 8: Hulton Archive/Getty Images. Page 12: Matt Carmichael/Getty Images. Page 20: Joe Capozio. Page 26: SpinnatoGallery.com. Pages 32, 74, 80, 96, 114, and insert: Courtesy of *Bass Player* magazine. Page 38: Peter Noble/Redfern. Page 44: John Stix; courtesy of *Bass Player* magazine. Page 56: Carles Roche; www.garywillis.com. Page 62: Judith Schiller; courtesy of Mark Egan. Page 68: Courtesy of Jimmy Haslip. Page 84: Courtesy of Bunny Brunel. Page 90: Leeann Bailey; courtesy of Steve Bailey. Page 102: Andrew Lepley/Redferns. Page 109–111: Exodus Almasude; courtesy of *Bass Player* magazine.

Library of Congress Cataloging-in-Publication Data is available upon request.

ISBN 978-0-87930-925-1

www.backbeatbooks.com

Contents

i . . . . *Foreword by Pino Palladino*

iii . . . . *Introduction*

PART 1: ROCK SLIDE

2	**1. JACK BRUCE**	by Jim Roberts and Chris Jisi
8	**2. STING**	by Vic Garabrini and Karl Coryat
12	**3. LES CLAYPOOL**	by Karl Coryat, Greg Isola, Chris Jisi, and Brian Fox
20	**4. PINO PALLADINO**	by Chris Jisi
26	**5. BAKITHI KUMALO**	by Greg Isola and Chris Jisi
32	**6. BILL WYMAN**	by Jim Roberts and Greg Isola
38	**7. MICK KARN**	by Chris Jisi, Jim Roberts, James Rotondi, and Karl Coryat

PART 2: JAZZ GIANTS

44	**8. JACO PASTORIUS**	by Chris Jisi, Bill Milkowski, Elton Bradman, and Scott Shiraki
56	**9. GARY WILLIS**	by Chris Jisi, Bill Leigh, Ed Friedland, and Anil Prasad
62	**10. MARK EGAN**	by Jim Roberts and Chris Jisi
68	**11. JIMMY HASLIP**	by Alexis Sklarevski, Ed Friedland, and Chris Jisi
74	**12. PERCY JONES**	by Sean Gerety and Chris Jisi
80	**13. ALAIN CARON**	by Bill Milkowski and Peter Murray
84	**14. BUNNY BRUNEL**	by Ed Friedland

PART 3: LIQUID LESSONS

90	**15. STEVE BAILEY**	
96	**16. MICHAEL MANRING**	
102	**17. MARCUS MILLER**	

107 . . . . *Appendix I: Repair and Maintenance*

113 . . . . *Appendix II: Fretting about the Fretless: Observations and Anecdotes from the Pros*

115 . . . . *Bibliography*

117 . . . . *Acknowledgments*

117 . . . . *Contributors*

To Jaco Pastorius and his select group of fellow bassists who have
found their voices on the fretless bass and spoken loudly to the rest of us

To my late parents, Connie and Bud, who always supported my musical
endeavors with love and pride

· · · · · · · · · ·

Foreword

I vividly remember one of my very first sessions in the late '70s. The producer, upon seeing me take my fretless Fender Precision Bass from its case, remarked, "You're not going to play *that*, are you?" Comments on subsequent sessions included, "Did they forget to put frets on it?" or "Couldn't you afford one with frets?" And my personal favorite, "It'll be nice when it's finished." But barbs and insults aside, the fretless bass is a beautiful, expressive instrument. It is equally at home in jazz and other instrumental styles, and in pop music, where its unique sound—especially in the upper register—can sit prominently in the mix, along with the lead vocal.

There are numerous techniques natural to the fretless, including vibrato, glissing up or down to a pitch, and sliding harmonics; but even when played without any added expression, the shape of a note is different from that of a fretted bass. Of course, for the enhanced sense of freedom of not being tied down by frets there is payback in the shape of responsibility. With bass usually being the foundation of the music, intonation is critical. Indeed, while playing fretless is rewarding, it is not the easy option.

To that end, this book offers sage advice from top players who have deeply studied the fretless bass and taken it to lofty heights. In the pages that follow, the author has collected a vast amount of valuable information on what is a relatively new instrument. Through Q&A interviews, music lessons with notation and tab, biographical material, gear lists, and selected discographies, bassists from a cross-section of genres share insight into how they have used the instrument to voice their individual styles. In addition, we hear from the most respected sources in the industry with regard to care, setup, and maintenance of the fretless.

From my own experience, Chris Jisi, in his role as *Bass Player* magazine's East Coast ears, has always gone to great lengths to provide in-depth analysis of my musical concepts and playing approach, as well as accurate notation when transcribing some of the lines I have recorded over the years. This comes from his genuine passion for the instrument, and as a bassist himself, his understanding of the many techniques and subtle nuances of the fretless bass guitar. So enjoy Chris's homage to the humble but noble fretless. Whether you're a beginner or advanced pro, I know you'll be enlightened both in mind and fingerboard as you navigate the material before you.

—Pino Palladino

Introduction

The fretless bass has been liberated! Forgive the play on words borrowed from Stanley Clarke's declaration about the bass itself, but it's true. The fretless may be the offspring of—and the key link between—the acoustic bass and the electric bass guitar, but it has more than come into its own. Sure, it combines the warmth, woody tone, and fingerboard freedom of the upright with the quick punchy response, sustain, and clarity of the electric bass. However, the growl and trademark "mwaah" sound of the fretless, and its highly expressive nature, have enabled it to stand apart from its father and older brother.

Like the very nature of the instrument itself, the fretless bass started on a questionable note. It took a full fifteen years after Leo Fender developed the first mass-produced electric bass guitar for the first official fretless bass to be introduced. Ampeg's AUB-1 (Ampeg Unfretted Bass) debuted in 1966 (along with their first fretted electric, the AEB-1); this was mostly because the company's acoustic bass-playing customers were having trouble fingering fretted Fenders. Rolling Stones bassist Bill Wyman had pulled the frets out of an inexpensive Japanese bass in 1961 and played it on various Stones hits—making him quite possibly the first notable, recorded fretless bassist. Still, the instrument wasn't raising a pulse among pluckers. Even Fender didn't introduce a fretless model until their sunburst fretless Precision Bass in 1970. But that would all change.

In the early '70s, a young Florida bassist named Jaco Pastorius pulled the frets out of his '62 Jazz Bass and epoxied the fingerboard. A solo album and sides with Weather Report and Joni Mitchell followed, and by 1976 the fretless era was under way. As the most imitated, influential, and revered electric bass player of all, Jaco obviously launched a legion of fret-removing fanatics among his followers. Inferior copycats fell by the wayside, but others heard the call—either inspired by Pastorius or coming upon the instrument on their own (Percy Jones, Alphonso Johnson, Fernando Saunders, Freebo, Marshall Jones, Boz Burrell, and Rick Danko among them). Before long, the instrument had established its own lyrical legacy. Top players like Jack Bruce and Sting brought visual as well as aural exposure, while radio-borne hits helmed by Pino Palladino, Bakithi Kumalo, and Tony Levin (for artists like Paul Young, Paul Simon, and Peter Gabriel) put the sound of the instrument in everyone's ears, making it instantly recognizable worldwide. More reflection, following Pastorius's tragic passing in 1987, led guitarist Pat Metheny to site the fretless tone of his late pal Jaco as the most pervasive sound in jazz to escape into the broader culture since Miles Davis's muted trumpet.

Here, well into the first decade of the new millennium, the fretless bass guitar has matured into a multi-faceted groove and solo machine—one that can be found in all corners and genres of the global music scene, manned by a multitude of monsters. As a contributing editor of *Bass Player* magazine since its 1989 inception, I've been fortunate enough to help cover much of the instrument's past, present, and future. This book is a compilation of the very best fretless interviews, lessons, and instrument maintenance guides that have appeared in *Bass Player* over the years. While by no means are all the important fretless players and concepts covered in these pages, the information and inspiration contained herein will more than enable you to educate yourself and begin the quest to find your own voice on the instrument—in the process, helping to ensure that fretless bassists everywhere will keep on slip-slidin' away.

—Chris Jisi

Part 1
Rock Slide

· · · · · · · · ·

JACK BRUCE

by Jim Roberts and Chris Jisi

The original Renaissance man of rock & roll, Jack Bruce (born May 14, 1943, in Glasgow, Scotland) didn't get to fretless bass until after his celebrated run with Cream. But for the pioneering power trio's heralded reunion, in 2005, Bruce's fretless played a key role.

Who were your early influences on bass?

I wanted to play jazz. There was Mingus, and not long after that, people like Charlie Haden and Scott LaFaro. There were a lot of things happening in jazz at that time.

When did you discover the electric bass?

That was in 1962. There was a guy called Roy Babbington, an English bass guitar player who was in a band called the 4 Macs. He was the first person I saw playing the instrument who made me think, Well, it's not all *that* bad. I had known about the bass guitar before then, but I was very much a jazz purist.

Then I got asked by [producer] Chris Blackwell to do a session, just when Island Records was starting up. It was a jazz session with a fine Jamaican guitar player called Ernest Ranglin, and he wanted bass guitar. So I went to a music shop and borrowed a Guild semi-acoustic bass. It had those nylon tapewound strings that kind of went "boink." I took that in and did the session.

What was your first impression of the bass guitar?

I fell in love with it. I thought, Wow, this is easy and it's *loud*. Wait till I play with Ginger! It was an instantaneous thing. Steve Swallow says the same kind of thing happened to him. Cream was playing at the Fillmore West in 1967, and Gary Burton's group, with Steve on acoustic bass, was on the bill with us. Steve saw me playing, and he tells me he went out the next day and got a bass guitar and never went back to the acoustic.

The bass guitar is a fine instrument on its own. The electric guitar is kind of a bastard instrument, but the bass guitar is a *real* instrument, a unique instrument. And I especially love playing fretless, as I've done for years now. I'm in love with the fretless, and I find it much more difficult to play a fretted bass now. The frets get in the way!

Aside from Roy Babbington, which bass guitarists caught your ear?

Before him, there hadn't been any. But 'round about the time I started playing bass guitar, I began to hear James Jamerson. Listening to those Tamla records, I began to see the possibilities of the bass guitar. [*Ed. Note: Motown records were issued in England on the Tamla label.*] It wasn't limited to playing root notes four to the bar; it could actually be a melody instrument—which it very much was in the hands of James.

There were a couple of other people around, too—there was a guy named Cliff Barton, who was the first person I saw playing fretless bass. Later, I wrote a song for him,

called "Over the Cliff"; it's on *Things We Like*. He was playing fretless with [English bluesman] Cyril Davies.

From your earliest recordings up to the present day, there's a certain consistency of sound. Even with all the different instruments you've used, it always sounds like Jack Bruce.

The sound comes from your brain and then from your fingers—that's the secret, I think. The difference in tone between two piano players such as Thelonious Monk and Tommy Flanagan is vast, for instance, yet they're both playing the same instrument. It's touch. It's what you *do* with the instrument.

What's your basic technique?

I pluck with my two right-hand fingers and occasionally my thumb. On the left hand, once I started playing short-scale basses in the '60s, I went from using upright technique, with no third finger, to using all four left-hand fingers. I've also gone back to studying the veena again. It's a two-hundred-year-old, sort of bass-like Indian instrument with a large gourd at one end, a beeswax fingerboard with brass frets that you move for your own tuning, four playing strings, and three drone strings. The sound is intense—it just fills a room. Much of my bass technique with Cream came from playing the veena during that time: going back and forth with the index finger, à la Jamerson or Chuck Rainey. I did that a lot for a tremolo effect.

When did you begin playing fretless?

For a 1976 tour with [drummer] Simon Phillips and [keyboardist] Tony Hymas. Dan Armstrong built me a short-scale bass with a Plexiglas body. It was sort of like going back to my upright roots, and ultimately, it made my approach more melodic. After that bass, I tried long-scale fretless basses by Aria and Spector, and eventually I found what he was looking for. I went into a music store in Germany, saw a Warwick bass, and bought it. The company found out that I had one, so they got in touch with me. I told them, "It's promising, but you need to do a little work." I made some suggestions for improving the balance, changing the pickups, and so on, and they came up with the instrument I'm using to this day.

How has your playing changed since Cream, and how did that affect the way you approached the bass parts in the reunion shows?

At the Royal Albert Hall shows I realized it has changed more than I ever thought. I found myself playing this sort of flamenco bass style [*laughs*] with strums and chords and drones, not just lines. It just kind of happened, as a way of fulfilling the role I feel I have in the band now. A good example is the solo sections on "N.S.U.," "Deserted Cities of the Heart," and "Badge." Because it's a trio, it's almost like I'm playing a big rhythm guitar—as opposed to the first time around with Cream, when I played a more lead bass style. I'm hoping to develop the concept further.

How did you choose your basses for the shows? Did you consider using your Gibson EB-3?

I had tried the EB-3 some years before, and I found the short scale length to be like playing a toy. I literally couldn't do it anymore—I was hitting wrong notes because it was just too small. I've been using my fretless Warwick forever; it's my favorite bass, and I've been playing Cream songs on it with my own band, so I knew I would stick with it in some capacity. As for the Gibson EB-1, I've just fallen in love with it over the years. It's got a real deep, woofy sound. I think I got it from [luthier] Dan Armstrong, and I had some work done on it to keep it in shape. Then when I was playing with Ringo Starr [in the late '90s], I discovered you just can't play a fretless on those old Beatles songs [laughs]. On tunes like "A Little Help from My Friends," Paul had a certain sound and feel on his Hofner, so I started playing the EB-1 to recreate that. With Cream, I was going to switch between the two, tune by tune—but that seemed silly, so I looked at the set list and decided to start on the EB-1 and switch to the Warwick halfway through, after "Rollin' and Tumblin'," where I just play harmonica. Also, I had suggested to Warwick that they make a special bass—a nod toward my old EB-3—to celebrate this event. We haven't gotten it quite right yet, but the prototype was onstage and can be seen in the DVD.

What did you think of how the band sounded at Royal Albert Hall?

I was astonished. It felt really fresh and natural—that was what amazed us all, from the start of rehearsals. It sounded different; it sounded like now. It reflected how much we've grown, and how much we brought back to the band from all the projects we've done. I would say, with certain reservations, that it's a better band now than it was then. Our time and feel is better and we've matured; we're not trying to prove anything to anyone or to each other. There's a lot more respect and honesty, in a way—and, not to get maudlin, but there's a lot of love as well. After one of the shows, Ginger said to me, "You are a great bass player after all." I couldn't believe it—he'd never once said that in all the years.

Musically, the band didn't make many changes to the forms of the songs, and you avoided the long improvisational sections that were a trademark of Cream shows.

We felt most of the songs were sort of carved in stone, and to change them made little sense. As for the solo sections, we wanted to improvise, but we didn't want to go too long. That was a thing of the time, and I don't think it would be valid now. We wanted to avoid a nostalgia trip, where we break out the Marshall stacks and the psychedelic clothes. We didn't want to be a tribute band to ourselves!

Some critics maintain that Cream's long jams in the '60s were self-indulgent and overshadowed the band's best side—the concise studio recordings of forward-thinking original songs.

I tend to agree. There were two sides to the band. Once we got to eight tracks on the second album, we saw the possibilities of the studio, with overdubs and my ability to play keyboards—while live, we saw the opportunity to achieve something completely different. Both sides were equally valid, when they worked. Ultimately, however, when they look back years from now, I believe Cream will be best remembered for the songs. In a sense, the band lost its way with the long jams, and that became a sort of albatross. It was our version of the Who smashing gear. They got tired of that quickly; we didn't get tired of it, but it got tedious. I'm sure there were times when Ginger thought, "Oh, now I've got to play this long drum solo."

What was your bass approach on Cream records?

Well, the great aspect of recording is you have some time to work out the bass lines. You're not improvising; it's sort of re-composition, if you like. You perfect the part on run-throughs. "Badge" is a good example; we had the whole day to get it down—it was the most number of takes we ever did. My goal was always to create a bass line where, if you took away or changed one note, the whole song would collapse. I tried to carve the part out of the music, like a statue, so that I knew it would last.

How about your approach during the live extended jams?

I would start off supporting Eric, all the while playing with Ginger, and then I would build and almost goad Eric to reach the heights of his playing—and when that happened, I would take off as well. Every song was different; if you think of the first live version of "Crossroads"—which was maybe the best example of what the band was like live then—we start up high and stay up high. On others, like

Jack Bruce Ex. 1

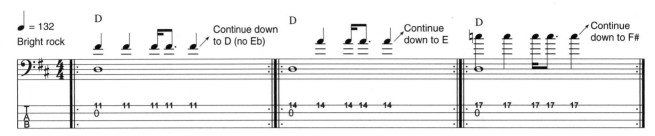

Jack Bruce Ex. 2

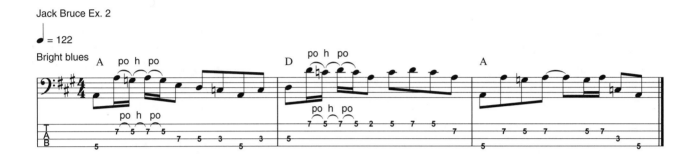

"Spoonful" [both from *Wheels of Fire*], we were trying to get this primeval, big vibration that just lasts. I would use fifths, chords, and countermelodies to fatten things up, because when Eric would play high, above my bass line, it left a lot of space in the middle. But, as I said, it was with more of a lead-bass attitude than my approach now.

That brings to mind the way you bent your strings by as much as a step and a half.

That was from seeing the way Eric played. When I got the EB-3, my thinking was: Well, it's a bass guitar. I wanted to emphasize the guitar aspect, which is why I put light-gauge La Bellas on it, for string bends. I was familiar with traditional forward-and-backward vibrato from playing cello and string bass, and I played the Fender VI with Graham Bond, to cover the guitar range when John McLaughlin left the band—but with Cream it was a whole new direction.

Any chance of an album of new Cream material?

It's something I'd love to do; it would be quite a challenge to try to create music that would stand up to the classic songs. I just don't know if it will happen, because we all feel the band is so special we don't want to do it that often, if we go on. I'd like to do it every now and again and just play somewhere, but we could do an album amidst that, and I'm going to suggest it.

BRUCE MUSIC

When faced once again with the bass role in the ultimate power trio, Jack Bruce did what comes naturally: he improvised. But in contrast to his unbridled lead and support lines in the original Cream, Bruce's experience told him his main responsibility was to hold down the groove and fill out the sonic spectrum. This he accomplished with radiance and invention via sophisticated moving lines, ringing pedals with upper-register chord tones, and less-is-more syncopated parts. The examples here refer to the performances on the Royal Albert Hall CD/DVD.

Ex. 1 illustrates Bruce's use of moving upper-register tones over an open D pedal—something he stumbled upon in Cream rehearsals—during Clapton's solo on "Deserted Cities of the Heart." Jack begins with a high F♯ and, playing the same rhythmic figure per bar, descends to F, E, and D over the next three measures. Next he jumps to a high A and descends chromatically to E over the next five measures (bar 2). Finally, he climbs to a high C and descends chromatically to F♯ over the next six measures (bar 3). Listen for some ear-grabbing fretless intervals!

In Ex. 2, Bruce revisits his original Cream "Crossroads" part on fretless, during Eric Clapton's solo. As in the original version, Jack adds hammered sixteenths in bars 1 and 2 for rhythmic excitement before returning to the classic unison riff/bass line in bar 3.

ESSENTIAL GEAR

Warwick fretless Jack Bruce Signature Model Thumb Bass; Gibson EB-1; S.I.T. medium nickel roundwounds; Hartke HA-5500 amps and VX810 and 115XL cabinets.

ESSENTIAL DISCOGRAPHY

With Cream (all on Polydor, except where noted): *Royal Albert Hall: London May 2, 3, 5 & 6, 2005* (CD & DVD), Reprise; *I Feel Free: Ultimate Cream*; *Cream Gold*; *BBC Sessions*; *Live Cream, Vols. 1 & 2*; *Goodbye*; *Wheels of Fire*; *Disraeli Gears*; *Fresh Cream*. **Solo albums:** *More Jack Than God*, Sanctuary; *Shadows in the Air*, Sanctuary; *Sitting on Top of the World*, Times Square; *Monkjack*, LocomotiveGT; *Cities of the Heart*, CMP; *Somethin' Els*, CMP; *A Question of Time*, Epic; *How's Tricks*, RSO; *Harmony Row*, Atco; *Things We Like*, Atco; *Songs for a Tailor*, Polygram. **With BBM:** *Around the Next Dream*, EMI. **With Kip Hanrahan** (both on American Clave): *All Roads Are Made of the Flesh*; *Vertical's Currency*. **With B.L.T.** (both on Capitol): *Truce*; *B.L.T.* **With Frank Zappa:** *Apostrophe*, Rykodisc. **With West, Bruce & Laing:** *Whatever Turns You On*, Windfall. **With Tony Williams Lifetime:** *Turn It Over*, Polydor. **With John Mayall:** *Looking Back*, Deram. **With Lou Reed:** *Berlin*, RCA. **With Carla Bley:** *Escalator Over the Hill*, ECM. **With Robin Trower: *Seven Moons*,** V-12.

STING

by Vic Garabrini and Karl Coryat

For Sting (born October 2, 1951, in Wallsend, Northumberland, England), his most fertile fretless period was with the Police, putting the sound in millions of ears and influencing scores of singing bassists.

How did you come to play fretless?

The Police had just arrived in America to promote "Roxanne," and we headed directly from the airport to the music shops on 48th Street. I remember being mesmerized by the steam hissing up through the gratings in the street as we wove through the Manhattan traffic; it looked exactly like hell, brimstone and all! Anyway, I went in and bought the first fretless I saw, a Fender Precision, and then I played it that night for an entire set at CBGB's—without practicing beforehand. There were no fret marks on it, so all I could do was try to keep a straight face and guess [*laughs*]. It was the first of many fretless incidents. At the end of the *Soul Cages* tour, I knocked the tuning pegs on my Ibanez fretless while going onstage. So I'm sliding up to the first note on the opening tune, going for the gliss, and this *bizarre* sound comes out. Ever try to re-tune a fretless in the middle of a song? That's why I don't play fretless on stage anymore—it's just a pain in the arse. But sometimes on a record I'll play a little fretless. Nowadays, I prefer the double bass to get that kind of sound.

Who were your key bass influences?

Jack Bruce, definitely. And Paul McCartney was a model in terms of being a bass player/songwriter. He had a good understanding of the bass's function, both melodically and contrapuntally. Anyone who plays bass and sings knows that most bass parts go against the rhythm. It's a counterpoint, and if you're singing on top of it you've got two lines weaving in and out of each other. Phil Lynott [of Thin Lizzy] was another influence.

Early on, how much work did you put into developing your playing?

I went through the Ron Carter school, and I spent years going through Ray Brown's double-bass book [*Ray Brown Bass Method*, Mail Box Music], just playing his scales and arpeggios. So I've paid my dues. I also spent a lot of time picking apart the Beatles. I love Paul's bass line on "She's a Woman" [*Past Masters, Volume One*, Capitol], for example. Plus James Jamerson's brilliant work at Motown—Carol Kaye's playing influenced me, as did a lot of individual songs, like "Rescue Me" by Fontella Bass, and Otis Redding's "Knock on Wood." I learned by listening. I'd often turn the record player up to 78 rpm so I could hear the bass lines rather than just feel them.

How did your reggae influence develop?

Well, in England we had reggae since its inception. Jamaica really wasn't the center of reggae—London was. In reggae there's a power shift toward the bass and away from the guitar, which was very attractive to me as a bassist. The

way bass is used in reggae, and particularly dub, is very radical. It's a revolutionary way of loading the rhythm of a bar, and it isn't easy to do. When a lot of people try to play reggae it ends up sounding like a cliché; you really have to get inside it.

I haven't mentioned Jaco yet, but he was another huge influence. He also shifted the power away from the guitar toward the bass in a revolutionary, astounding way. Who would have thought to play a chromatic Charlie Parker tune, "Donna Lee," on bass?

When people talk about your style, the concept of space always comes up. How conscious are you of putting space into a line?

It's an instinct with me. That partly has to do with singing in the gaps, and partly with the economy of music. For me, the sound is only half of music—the space between the notes is also vitally important. As musicians, all we do is create a frame for silence, because silence is the perfect music. But I'm perfectly happy to play eight to the bar on the root, chorus after chorus. I just want to pump the band along, drive it, and give it a safe home.

When you write, do the bass parts come after the melody or along with it?

I've never thought much about the bass parts while I was writing, to be honest. I just make them up on the spot once I've written the song, with an eye towards being able to sing at the same time. Other times, I've written the song on bass. If you've got the right riff, the song can just write itself. That's what happened with "Walking on the Moon" [*Regatta de Blanc*]. I wish I could find another one of those every day: a simple, easy, three-note or four-note riff. The whole song is based around its cadence, and I'm very proud of that.

Do you prefer to record your bass direct?

Yes, I usually plug right into the board. In the Police we'd all play in the same room, and all I'd hear was Andy's guitar—which needed to be loud to get that natural distortion—and Stewart's drums. But I hate the sound of a bass coming through headphones—it sounds like a mechanical fart. So nowadays I play in the control room, where I can get a warmer sound and can mix and adjust the other instruments to approximate how they'll sound on the record.

You sometimes doubletrack your bass lines, don't you?

I often use the double bass over the original electric bass lines, because the double bass has overtones that you *feel*—a big subliminal undercurrent of sound. We used that combination on "All This Time" on *The Soul Cages*. Sometimes I use an old Italian bass, but I often use the Z

Sting Ex. 1

♩ = 168

Reggae rock

Bass. It's a Van Zalinge electric standup I got in Holland a decade ago, when the Police were recording *Zenyatta Mondatta*. You can hear it on the original "Don't Stand So Close to Me." I also used the Z Bass on "Every Little Thing She Does Is Magic." On *Synchronicity*, I combined it with a Precision fretless on "Wrapped Around Your Finger" and with a Steinberger on "King of Pain."

You change your plucking-hand technique from song to song, something a lot of bassists don't do.

Over the last ten years I've adapted a classical guitar technique called apoyando, where you play with the fingers underneath the thumb. I don't know many bassists who do that. Sometimes I use my thumb and dampen the strings with the side of my hand, and I use just my fingers for certain things, too. I don't use a plec [pick] very often, except when I want to get an effect. I'll try just about anything, but I especially like to chug along on a dampened bass. I'm still willing to learn; I'm still a student. That's my only ambition, really: to remain a student of music. I never want to think I know everything now—because the more I know, the less I'm sure about.

STING MUSIC

Sting has all the qualities of a great bass player: he's melodic, inventive, rhythmically interesting, and he can make a tune develop and grow as it progresses. A great example is his fretless P-Bass part on "Every Little Thing She Does Is

Magic," from the fourth Police Album, *Ghost in the Machine*. After laying down half-note roots and thirds in the verse, Sting leads into the chorus with two busier bars and a cool slide. The first two measures of the chorus establish an interesting pattern: he plays on the *one* and *four* of each measure, but not the *two* and *three*, a nod to his reggae influences that gives the section both space and movement. Ex. 1 is inspired by and similar to the last two measures of the verse and the first two measures of the chorus.

ESSENTIAL GEAR

Fretless '54 Fender Precision; fretted '54 P-Bass; '62 Jazz Bass; fretless Spector NS2; fretless Ibanez Musician; fretless Ibanez Roadstar II; Z-bass electric upright; '80s Steinberger; Rotosound Swing Bass mediums; DR Lo-Riders; Alembic FX-1 preamp; Carver power amps; Clair Bros. speakers.

ESSENTIAL DISCOGRAPHY

Solo albums (all on A&M): *Sacred Love*; *Brand New Day*; *Mercury Falling*; *Ten Summoner's Tales*; *The Soul Cages*; . . . *Nothing Like the Sun*; *Bring On the Night*; *Dream of the Blue Turtles*. **With the Police** (all on A&M): *Every Breath You Take* (compilation); *Synchronicity*; *Ghost in the Machine*; *Zenyatta Mondatta*; *Regatta de Blanc*; *Outlandos d'Amour*. **With John McLaughlin**: *Promise*, Verve. **With Black Eyed Peas**: *Monkey Business*, A&M.

LES CLAYPOOL

by Karl Coryat, Greg Isola, Chris Jisi, and Brian Fox

Dubbed an anti-bass hero, Les Claypool (born September 29, 1963, in Richmond, California) stopped the early-'90s bass world in its tracks, manning his fretless six-string with Primus. Although he has since fronted other bands on a variety of basses, the fretless remains a vital part of his fearless flights of fancy.

Who was your earliest bass influence?

Geddy Lee with Rush. Geddy was God; there was nobody better than him. He was just the best.

How did you learn his parts?

I didn't. I listened to players like Geddy and Chris Squire and watched them in concert, and I got ideas from that. But I don't think I ever learned a Rush tune all the way through. I'd put on Rush records and play to them, but I didn't have an amp, so I was just moving my fingers around. When I saw my first Rush concert, I spent the whole time watching Geddy's hands.

How did you discover funk?

One day, a friend of mine said, "Geddy Lee is good, but he's nothing compared to Stanley Clarke and Larry Graham." I told him he was crazy, even though I didn't know who those guys were. Then I saw Stanley's *I Want to Play for Ya* [Portrait/Sony] in a record store. I bought it, and it blew my mind. I also saw Louis Johnson on [the TV show] *Don Kirshner's Rock Concert*, saw him go *bang-bippety-bip-bang*, and thought, "Man, that's the coolest thing!" By my junior year, I was getting way into all the funk players. Guys would give me shit and call me "Disco Les" because I was playing all this funk stuff.

Around my senior year, I bought an Ibanez Musician EQ bass. I had always wanted a Rickenbacker before, but then I decided the Rickenbacker was no longer the cool bass to have. I hung around Leo's [music store] in Oakland all the time; they had tons of new and used stuff. One day, I saw a Carl Thompson piccolo bass sitting there. I had stared at the photo in *I Want to Play for Ya* where Stanley had all his basses lined up, and a couple of them were Carl Thompsons. I always thought, "Man, that sure is an ugly bass." I picked up the one in the store, though, and I couldn't believe it—it was so easy to play. Suddenly there were a lot of things I could play that I couldn't play on my Ibanez. I used to test basses by trying to play "Roundabout," and it was pretty easy on the Carl Thompson. I went home, and I begged and pleaded with my mom for the rest of the money I needed to buy that bass. She lent me some, and I went back and bought it. It's still my main four-string.

In the '80s, it wasn't cool to have a fancy-woodwork custom bass; it was cooler to have a pink one or something the color of toothpaste. So people were constantly giving me shit for having a bass that looked like some weird piece of furniture.

How did you develop your right-hand dexterity?

One of the big things I decided to do when I was starting out was to play with three fingers. A lot of guys play with two fingers, so I figured if I played with three, I could be faster. When you're young, that's the goal: to be fast. I still use three fingers most of the time—going *ring, middle, index, ring, middle, index*—depending on how sore my fingers are. Sometimes I'll mix it up and favor certain fingers over others.

Where did you pick up the strumming technique?

From Stanley Clarke, because of songs like "School Days." The first time I saw Stanley shoot the ol' chords—he'd start at the top and go *pow!* [*mimes strumming and sliding a chord down the fingerboard*]—I thought that was way cool, and I decided to do it. It hurt like hell when I first started.

Did Stanley also inspire you to start slapping?

Yeah, him and Louis Johnson. Louis's right arm would go way out away from the bass. Stanley, though, used minimal hand movement, and I was always into the minimal hand-movement thing. A friend of mine told me your thumb should just *graze* the string and rest against the next one, as opposed to whapping the string and bouncing off it. My thumb got pretty fast, since I was more into thumbing than plucking.

One thing that helped me a ton, probably more than anything in my career, was playing with a group called the Tommy Crank Band. The other guys were all in their twenties and thirties, and I was nineteen. I had been playing fusion, and when I played with them the first time I was like *bloobilla-bloobilla-bloobilla!* They said, "Cool," and I got the gig. I had to learn all these blues and R&B tunes; we played everything from James Brown to John Cougar, everywhere from biker bars to weddings. I had never learned any of these songs, so I just asked what key they were in and did my own interpretations. A lot of the time I overplayed, and everyone else in the band was always clamping down on me to mellow out. By playing these tunes four hours a night, three to five nights a week, my groove got really good, and I learned to improvise and pull off songs we hadn't even rehearsed.

Were you influenced by other rock bass players at that time?

I always wanted to play bass parts *and* rhythm guitar parts. I never really listened to other bass players that much. To this day, people come up and say, "Hey, what do you think of Jaco's blah blah blah," and I'll go, "Never heard it in my life." Or, "You haven't heard Jonas Hellborg?!" and I say, "Nope." I feel bad because there are a lot of great players out there I haven't heard. I was just never into "player" records; I'm much more apt to buy a Tom Waits CD instead of one by a bass player. I'm also more apt to get into drummers than bass players. I play the drums a lot; I like playing drums. On drums, you can kick back; nobody fucks with you, and you can just play. It's physical, and you can get your aggressions out. It's funny—I enjoy playing drums more than bass, but I'm better at bass.

When did you get your Carl Thompson six-string?

I was doing a demo at NAMM for ADA, and this guy came up to me and said, "Oh, you play a Carl Thompson bass? Look at this." He whipped out this amazing Carl Thompson six-string fretless. After that I knew I had to have a six-string, but I wasn't sure if I wanted a fretless.

I didn't actually get my six until just before we started *Sailing the Seas of Cheese*. We were on tour in New York, and I tracked down Carl Thompson. I told him I was interested in a six-string; he was impressed that I had been playing his bass for years and loving it. A little while later, he started hearing my name around, so he called me and said he'd start building me a bass if I sent a deposit.

I couldn't decide whether I wanted a fretted or a fretless. But I was getting to a point with my four-string where it was like a stalemate; I was getting bored with it. I needed something that would just blow things wide open, so I decided to go for the fretless six-string.

Carl told me he was going to make the best bass he'd ever built in his life. He basically made a butcher block out of all these different pieces of wood, and then he cut the body shape out of it. He called it the "Rainbow" bass. Apparently it almost killed him to make it; he had a bad sinus problem, and all the dust was making it worse. And I was saying, "Carl, I need the bass before we start our next record," so he had to rush—he even had to go to the hospital at one point. But he finished it on his birthday, and the serial number is his date of birth.

When I got the bass, I thought, "Ohmigod—what have I done?" It was so much more difficult to play. I was used to my four-string's 32" scale, and all of a sudden I had this big hunk of wood with a 36" scale and no frets. When I tried to play chords they all sounded like shit, and I couldn't move around very well. But I kept playing it and playing it, to the point where I felt comfortable on it.

Your influence in the bass world is undeniable. How much do you think about your status as a bass player?

I'm never trying to be a bass superhero, that's for sure. I think in terms of images and songs, not in terms of how groundbreaking a bass part can be. I do love the fact that there are kids who look at me the way I looked at Geddy Lee and Tony Levin and Larry Graham. That's marvelous and wonderful, and sometimes it can be incredibly touching, but it's not something I think about when I'm playing.

Do you think about bass first when you're writing?

The bass is what I start with if it's the instrument that happens to be sitting there. When I've written stuff on guitar, it's been because I've been playing guitar when something interesting came out. "The Toys Go Winding Down" [from Primus' *Frizzle Fry*] is a good example. I wrote that dickita-dickita-dickita part on guitar, and it's just because I was practicing my heavy metal riffs [*laughs*]. I thought it sounded good and wondered how it would sound on bass. That's how I often do stuff. I didn't want to just say, "Larry, here's your guitar part," so I played the guitar part on bass.

I also had Carl Thompson do some work on my "Rainbow" [fretless six-string] bass. I quit using it when Brain joined the band because it had just become so difficult to play. So I had Carl reshape the neck and lighten the headstock considerably. When all is said and done, the instrument you pick up most often, the one you feel compelled to play, is the one that's comfortable—the one that sits on your body well when you're sitting in front of the TV. That bass was not like that; it was always very awkward, and I always had to force myself to play it. But it's great if you want a big, loping, Tony Levin-type part, with thick, girthy half-notes.

Is the "Rainbow" bass as heavy as it looks?

It actually doesn't weigh all that much, but it was very top-heavy because the tuners were so big. So Carl put different tuners on it and reshaped the neck a bit, and it's way better now. It's incredible how great it feels. He's a pretty ingenious guy.

Is technique something you still have to think about?

I still sit down in front of the TV with my bass and noodle around, just to keep things lubricated. I need to as I get older. I never used to practice before gigs or anything. Tod Huth, our old guitarist, used to warm up completely before every show, but I never did. I'd just sit around drinkin' beers and smokin' weed. But as I get older, I do find that I play better if I keep the gears in shape.

My most intense playing to date has been on the road with the Frog Brigade. I was constantly challenging the

Les Claypool Ex. 1

♩ = 118

Funk rock

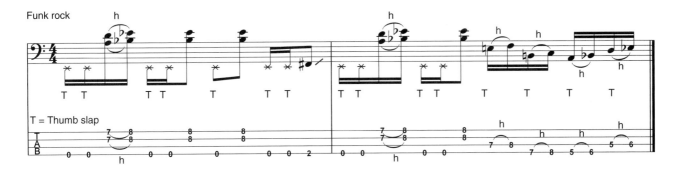

T = Thumb slap

Les Claypool Ex. 2

♩ = 208

Funk rock

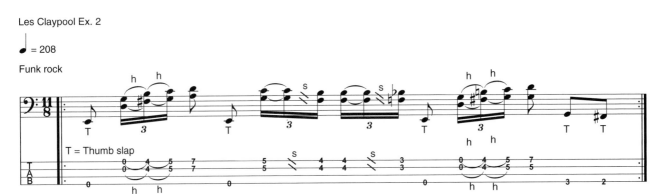

T = Thumb slap

band, and myself, with material. We'd play Pink Floyd's *Animals* from start to finish, or we'd learn new tunes every day. These were just ways to stay fresh, because out on the road, you need to keep up your chops. But coming together with Larry and Tim is a completely different thing. For example, it never occurs to me to do much tapping with Frog Brigade, mainly because there are so many guys up there. There just isn't much space for that kind of playing.

For years, you couldn't read a description of Primus' music that didn't include the word "sloppy." But you guys are playing great these days. No one new to the music would ever describe Primus as sloppy.

It's funny; I've read that stuff in *Bass Player* [*laughs*], criticizing my intonation and whatnot, but honestly I've never gotten the "sloppy" thing. If anything, people are more often surprised at how tightly we've always played together. A lot of that, of course, is because of Tim Alexander, who is a very precise player. Even when we're really stretching on something, you can rarely tell that we're still a band that doesn't rehearse much. And a huge part of that is because of Tim.

CLAYPOOL MUSIC

Les Claypool's bass lines tend to repeat in one- or two-bar phrases, with only small variations from measure to measure. His parts feature lots of muted, thumbed, popped, and strummed notes, and he favors barred fourths and root-fifth-octave chords. One constant? Les stands firmly in groove mode, even when he's at his most tyrannical on the fingerboard.

Ex. 1, from "Pudding Time" (*Frizzle Fry*), is a fairly simple introduction to Claypooldom. Mute the E string with a left-hand finger or thumb, barre the top notes with your index finger, and strum the top two strings with your right-hand fingernails in a quick, downward motion. For the slide, have your left hand moving as you slap the string; that way, the slide will begin on an indefinite pitch.

The 11/8 time signature of "Eleven" from *Sailing the Seas of Cheese* can be very difficult to count. But in this tune, the beats are strongly grouped in an easy-to-grasp way: *one-two-three, one-two-three, one-two-three, one-two*. (That's why the eighth-notes are grouped as such in the notation.) Ex. 2 illustrates the repeating pattern. The strums should be done strongly, to emphasize the beats they fall on (the "pa-pa" of the "oom-pa-pa" feel); the hammered notes should be

Les Claypool Ex. 3

♩ = 120

Funk rock

RFT = Right-hand index and middle finger tap
LHS = Left-hand slap

Les Claypool Ex. 4

♩ = 140

Funk shuffle

T = Thumb slap

Les Claypool Ex. 5

♩ = 140

Funk shuffle

merely embellishments. For the slides, fret the D string with your middle finger and the G string with your ring finger.

It's possible to play Ex. 3 from *Sailing*'s "Jerry Was a Race Car Driver" on a fretted four-string by moving all the notes down an octave, but it's harder to execute and doesn't sound as good. In this line, none of the notes is plucked—they're all either hammered or pulled off. The first A♭, for instance, is played simply by hammering the note onto the fretboard (as are the B♭ on two and the D♭ on the *and* of four). The ghost notes are produced simply by slapping the left hand down on the strings without letting any of the actual notes sound.

Examples 4 and 5 are from "Jackalope," off of *The Big Eyeball in the Sky*, by Colonel Claypool's Bucket of Bernie Brains. Ex. 4 is the main slapped shuffle groove that emanates from Les's famed fretless Carl Thompson 6. Note the cool double-stop hammer-on in bar 1 of Ex. 4. Ex. 5 contains the weird walking line in the bridge, which is framed by Bernie Worrell's "out" organ chords.

Turning to Primus's *Animals Should Not Try to Act Like People*, Ex. 6 shows Les's trippy main fretless groove from "Mary the Ice Cube." Check out how he uses slides and vibrato to heighten the black-light effect. Ex. 7 captures the

Les Claypool Ex. 6

♩ = 122

Trippy rock   Am⁷

Les Claypool Ex. 7

♩ = 118

Funk rock   D

LHT = Left-hand tap
RHT = Right-hand tap

two-handed tapped groove 5:01 into "The Carpenter and the Dainty Bride." Les taps the low D with his left index finger, while tapping the high E and A with his right index finger and middle finger, respectively.

ESSENTIAL GEAR

Carl Thompson "Rainbow" six-string fretless; Thompson fretted six; Thompson fretted (with whammy bar) and fretless four-strings; '72 Rickenbacker; Spector NS-2 electric upright; Kay upright; Dean Markley strings; ADA MP1 guitar preamp; MESA/Boogie Bass 400 Plus head and two MESA/Boogie 2x15 cabinets.

ESSENTIAL DISCOGRAPHY

Solo albums: *Purple Onion*, Prawn Song; *Les Claypool and the Holy Mackerel Presents Highball with the Devil*, Interscope. **With Primus:** (on Interscope) *Animals Should Not Try to Act Like People*; *AntiPop*; *Rhinoplasty*; *The Brown Album*; *Tales from the Punchbowl*; *Pork Soda*; *Miscellaneous Debris*; *Sailing the Seas of Cheese*; (on Caroline) *Frizzle Fry*; *Suck on This*. **With the Fearless Flying Frog Brigade** (both on Prawn Song): *Live Frogs: Set 2*; *Live Frogs: Set 1*. **With Oysterhead:** *The Grand Pecking Order*, Elektra. **With Sausage:** *Riddles Are Abound Tonight*, Interscope.

PINO
PALLADINO

Simply put, Pino Palladino (born October 17, 1957, in Cardiff, Wales) was the most popular and influential of all the post-Pastorius fretless bassists, thanks to his vibrant parts with Paul Young and Don Henley. He has gone on to become one of the most versatile and in-demand bassists on the planet, plucking for everyone from Paul Simon and the Who to D'Angelo and John Mayer.

Many of your ideas seemed to come together on Paul Young's *No Parlez*. What were the key events in that process?

While I was on tour with Jools Holland, I happened to visit Sam Ash Music in New York City, where I purchased a fretless '79 Music Man StingRay bass. I'd owned a fretless Precision previously, but it hadn't really grabbed me. When I got back to London, a Welsh drummer friend of mine, Chris Slade, had left a message saying that Gary Numan was looking for a fretless bass player and that I should come down and audition. So I took the Music Man and went over and played through a bunch of his songs. They all had simple changes, which gave me a lot of room to try different things. I ended up touring and doing a record with him called *I Assassin*. That was great, because it was the first time I got to express myself in the studio with something other than typical bass parts. I remember hearing the sound of the fretless on a playback and thinking, "Hmmm—there's something here for me."

Around that time, Paul Young was about to record his first album. My girlfriend—who's now my wife—was singing backup for him, and Laurie Latham, who'd worked on Gary's album, was producing. Laurie called me in to help out on a Marvin Gaye cover called "Wherever I Lay My Hat (That's My Home)." All that was down was a drum machine, keyboard pads, and a guide vocal. Laurie asked me to play something melodic on the fretless as a lead-in to the vocal. I tried to give it a sort of Jaco vibe, which seemed to work out well. We did four or five more tracks, and then I went home and forgot all about it. When I heard the mixes a while later, I was in shock. The bass was so loud; I thought, "They've got to be joking. What will people think?" But there was an affinity between the voice and bass, and that was really the start of it. When "Wherever I Lay My Hat" became a hit in Europe, word of mouth spread, and I got calls to do sessions with people like David Gilmour, Joan Armatrading, and Go West. It was amazing.

How did you hook up with Don Henley?

That's an odd story. I had recorded an album with a singer called Nick Heyward, and his manager told me that Don had heard the album and was interested in hiring me. I took it with a pinch of salt and didn't do anything for about two months. Finally, I plucked up the courage, rang him, and explained the situation. He said he didn't recall telling anyone that—but he also said the he and his partner, [guitarist/producer] Danny Kortchmar, were familiar with my playing and would be interested in doing some recording with me.

It seems that your style reached its full fruition on Paul Young's 1985 album, *The Secret of Association*.

The key factor was that we were given a much bigger budget. That enabled us to be a lot more indulgent with time, especially with regard to the bass parts. Most of the tracks were laid down before I played on them, and then we went through and tried different things. By "we" I mean myself; keyboardist/musical director Ian Kewley, who had a great vision; and [producer] Laurie Latham, again, applying his concept of bass featured with voice and its placement in the mix. Those two, along with Paul, helped me to create what's on the record.

What makes your Music Man unique?

Well, there are countless fretless basses available now with brighter-sounding polyester-coated fingerboards and PJ or JJ pickups that offer more tones, but the Music Man, with the bass and treble knobs turned midway and my plucking fingers right over the pickup, has this one versatile, warm sound that speaks to me. Also, I've always felt that the bridge-pickup sound belongs to Jaco.

How did you come to use an octaver?

While working with Laurie for an artist called Jackie Brooks, I cut a bass part, and one of us got the idea to double a couple of notes an octave higher. It sounded so good Laurie had me double the whole part that way. I figured there must be an effect pedal I could get to play the higher octave. I bought the Boss OC-2 and realized I had to do it the other way around—play up an octave. That was a plus, because it helped me learn the fingerboard up high, and it enabled me to play some outfront lines while retaining the bottom end. It also put me in the mind of Stevie Wonder's synth-bass playing.

Who are the key influences on your bass approach?

Early on it was James Jamerson, Stevie Wonder's keyboard bass, Danny Thompson, a great upright bass player in England—I used to sit transfixed in clubs watching him play slides, double-stops, and harmonics—and Norman Watt-Roy of Ian Dury and the Blockheads.

The key players for me would be Jamerson, Stevie, Jaco Pastorius, of course, Anthony Jackson—his recordings with Chaka Khan in particular kill me—Michael Henderson, Larry Graham, Rocco Prestia, Marcus Miller, and Bootsy—his part on James Brown's "Talkin' Loud and Sayin' Nothing" is one of my all-time favorites. Michael's solo album *Going Places* [Capitol] was a huge inspiration; he's similar to Jamerson, but with his own take on it. I also loved the early fusion stuff with Stanley and Jaco; a lot of it was funky, like George Duke's *The Aura Will Prevail* [BASF] with Alphonso Johnson, and Lenny White's *Venusian Summer* [Nemperor], with the late Doug Rauch—he played some stinky funk that blew me away.

Can you elaborate on your right- and left-hand techniques?

Mostly I pluck with two fingers on my right hand. I started that way on bass, probably because of the classical-guitar lessons and because the sound appealed to me. Occasionally I'll use the third finger on, say, a ballad, because I can get a warm tone with it. My thumb technique, which I don't use much anymore, is the basic slap-and-pull approach. I've also been using a muted technique where I dampen the strings with my right palm and pluck with the thumb; I used that on "Stop On By" [Paul Young, *Other Voices*]. With the left hand, I usually use finger-a-fret spacing, again from the classical guitar, although my vibrato on the fretless is anything but classical. I tend to move my whole hand back and forth as opposed to rolling the fingertip.

Can you offer any tips for achieving good intonation on fretless?

I never think about intonation, because when I do that's when I have trouble! When I first started playing the Music Man, I thought to myself, "This is amazing—I can even play chords in tune." It was like the instrument was built for my hands. It has no fret lines, but I do use the dot markers on the side of the neck. One thing I always try to do is think ahead, as far as positions and shifts, because there are so many ways to get from one note to another. It's not like playing on a fretted bass, where you can take your eye off matters more readily. The fretless is more spontaneous; the one thing you can't plan exactly is when to apply vibrato, or when to slide into certain notes, because that's intrinsic in the music. That's where a great vocal performance is invaluable—you react to a sung note or phrase.

When you're recording a track, how do you decide when to step forward musically?

I find there are two methods. When I listen to the demo, or when we first play the song through, I'll sense if it requires a straight-away part that can be completed within a few takes. Then I'll think about whether I'm going to play with the kick drum pattern or against it, and if there's room to add any little melodic things, chords, harmonics, whatever. The other approach involves putting down a basic track with the drummer or drum machine, and then going back to find if there's room to add something nice. Usually, I deal with the latter method, but I really enjoy the former, too—

especially when I'm working with a great drummer who can inspire you to do incredible things on the spot.

How do you come up with parts? Do you think in terms of chord changes, melodies, or rhythmic ideas?

I just wait for something to come into my head. Sometimes I let the track play without any bass a few times to see if I can imagine the bass line. It's instinctive; when you hear a great song you get an idea of what it needs in the bass line. I think most players have that ability deep down, but it's a matter of having the confidence to not overplay, to not have an ego that says I have to put my stamp on the track—instead, just trying to fit into the song. When you're playing along with a song, there's a point where you say, Yeah, this is the right thing to do, and it just feels right. In that scenario it's almost always a matter of coming from a place of economy: playing less and adding as needed, as opposed to being busy and having to cut back. The song itself is what's going to make a track happen, and the less you can do to make it work, the better. I like that kind of Zen approach: if I can play one note and make the song work, I'm happy to do that. By the same token, if the drum beat is really grooving and it needs more from the bass, then I'll obviously go for something more adventurous.

Technically, there's a degree of musical knowledge in the equation—knowing the changes and being aware that you can play something nice over this Em9 chord coming up. There are certain places in a song where each musician gets a little spark and thinks, "Well, I can put something special in here—this spot is where I can do my thing." The rest of the time it's a probably a good idea to just keep it simple.

Part of what makes your fills jump out is the way they're phrased. Do you get into a separate mindset to play fills as opposed to a groove part?

Yes. It's almost like I'm playing the support line and occasionally I feel like singing something. I find when I go to the upper register and play something that's going to stand out a little, it's a natural for me to phrase it in a more vocal, soloistic fashion. I don't sing out loud with the licks, but I do feel them vocally. It's a matter of being aware that you have to let go of holding down the root and locking with the drums, and step into a different frame of mind to get it to come out more loose and relaxed. Musically, I hear notes other than the root that fit with the chords. When I play bass I'm always trying to hear what else could work. Other things just fall under the fingers nicely, like I know this pentatonic lick will fit here, I've used it before, but maybe I can alter it slightly.

In more recent years you haven't played as much fretless. How do you reflect on that era?

I feel good about it overall. Occasionally I'll hear a Paul Young or Don Henley track in a store and it sounds real good to me—I'm proud of what I did. Sometimes I even get the inkling, "Man, maybe I'll just play everything on fretless again!" [*Laughs.*]

Did having such a strong style eventually paint you into a corner, making you a victim of your own success?

For sure; most session musicians go through a cycle like that. There definitely was a time when people had enough of the fretless sound. Plus, I was sick of it before anyone else was! I'd hear other people trying to do me, and while it was flattering in a sense, I would mostly feel embarrassed. Toward the end I was getting so jaded with the whole front-of-the-mix thing and coming up with sub-hooks. I was starting to repeat myself. I'd think, Whoa, I've got to get some other shit going; this is driving me crazy! Fortunately, the downturn didn't really cost me work; I stayed busy.

What do you retain from your fretless approach in your current fretted style?

A great deal. Playing so many fretless bass lines that were featured as important parts of songs gave me the confidence I have today to try ideas and step out a little. Technique-wise, I keep the phrasing and vibrato aspects in mind, although I was using vibrato and moving my hand on fretted bass before I ever got a fretless—in the vein of Paul Jackson and Abe Laboriel. And I still get to record on fretless; I've played a Stratus with black nylon strings on some demos for D'Angleo; I played a rare old fretless Ampeg AUB-1—the one with the scroll headstock—that Brian Eno had at the studio on "That's Me," from Paul Simon's *Surprise* CD; and I overdubbed my Music Man on John Mayer's "Slow Dancing in a Burning Room" [from *Continuum*].

Considering your more recent success as a key member of bands like the Who, D'Angelo, Simon and Garfunkel, and the John Mayer Trio, can you ever see yourself changing gears and becoming a one-band guy for a while?

I could see that happening, but then again I love so many different styles of music that what I enjoy most is playing in various musical circles. I'm just happy and very fortunate to be able to ride the wave.

PALLADINO MUSIC

Pino Palladino's fretless work encompasses the entire bass spectrum, from slides, smears, and harmonics to singing melodic phrases to octaver-aided keyboard-style lines to crisp slapped passages and staccato sixteenth-note grooves. This range is especially apparent in his work with Paul Young. The examples that follow are typical of his parts with the '80s chart-topping crooner. Ex. 1 and 2 are inspired by Pino's fretless work on tunes like "Everytime You Go Away." Ex. 1 recalls Pino's double-stop verse fills, beginning with ear-grabbing fourths and ending with a tasty double-stop that exploits the seven and flat nine. Ex. 2 illustrates a typically classic "Pino-ism," a memorable sub-hook (bar 2) that answers the vocal.

Ex. 3 shows a typical chorus-fade line Pino might play on his Pedulla Buzz Bass plus octave pedal on tunes like Paul Young's "I'm Gonna Tear Your Playhouse Down." Pino completely alters his original line and pumps sixteenths that outline a Gm11 arpeggio in bar 1, and a finger-twisting variation in bar 3. Finally, Ex. 4 recalls the kind of quarter-note stroll and savory fill Pino might play on Young's cover of the Bobby Womack/Rufus tune "Stop On By."

ESSENTIAL GEAR

Basses: '79 Music Man StingRay four-string; '63 P-Bass; '61 P-Bass; Pino Palladino signature P-Bass; Fender Jaguar Bass; Moon Larry Graham Signature Jazz Bass; '96 Lakland 55-94 Deluxe five-string; Rotosound Swing Bass medium and La Bella heavy flatwound string; Ashdown, Epifani, and Phil Jones amps; Boss OC-2 Octave Pedal.

ESSENTIAL DISCOGRAPHY

With Paul Young (all on Columbia): *Other Voices*; *The Secret of Association*; *No Parlez*. **With Don Henley** (both on Geffen): *The End of the Innocence*; *Building the Perfect Beast*. **With John Mayer** (both on Columbia): *Continuum*; *Try!* **With the Who:** *Wire and Glass: Six Songs from a Mini-Opera*, Polydor. **With Paul Simon:** *Surprise*, Warner Bros. **With D'Angelo:** *Voodoo*, Virgin. **With Eric Clapton:** *Journeyman*, Reprise. **With Herbie Hancock:** *Possibilities*, Vector. **With Erykah Badu:** *Mama's Gun*, Motown. **With Tears For {Au: Is the capital F in For part of the band's style?} Fears:** *The Seeds of Love*, Polygram. **With Roy Hargrove Presents The RH Factor:** *Hard Groove*, Verve. **With Oleta Adams:** *Circle of One*, Polygram. **With Michael McDonald:** *Blink of an Eye*, Warner Bros. **With B.B. King:** *Deuces Wild*, MCA. **With Seal** (both on Sire): *Seal* (1991); *Seal* (1994). **With Go West:** *Go West*, Chrysalis. **With Common:** *Electric Circus*, MCA. **With Gary Numan:** *I Assassin*, Beggars Banquet.

BAKITHI KUMALO

by Greg Isola and Chris Jisi

Bakithi Kumalo (Bah-gee-tee Koo-mah-low; born May 10, 1956, in Alexandra, Soweto Township, outside of Johannesburg, South Africa) gave the fretless a world-music flavor via his ear-grabbing displays of lyricism and deep groove with Paul Simon. He retains those qualities on all his basses to this day.

• •

"It's been many years since I recorded in South Africa, but I still remember the first time I heard the enormous, *incredible* sound Bakithi got out of his bass—almost like a horn, but so primal."
—Paul Simon 1996

Under African Skies

Born in the South African township of Alexandra on May 10, 1956, Kumalo grew up in nearby Soweto, surrounded by music. "My mother had a band," he explains. "She was a singer, and my dad played guitar. My uncle had a band, too; he was a saxophone player, and I was always checking him out when he was practicing." Early on, Bakithi did more than just listen. "One time my uncle's bass player got drunk and couldn't make it for a wedding gig. I knew the set—it consisted of simple I–IV–V songs and traditional South African music—and my uncle asked, 'Can you handle it?' 'Oh, yes! I'm ready,' I said. I was seven years old; the bass was so heavy, and my fingers were *small*. But I had to play, and I held the groove for them."

After formally joining his uncle's band, little Bakithi made the rounds, hitting up every local musician he could find for information and instruction. "I was a troublemaker," he laughs. "There were a lot of good musicians around home back then. At all of their rehearsals, the bass players would be saying, 'Oh, no—here he comes again!'"

Despite his uncle's chiding, Kumalo was determined to become a professional musician. When he was ten years old, the lure of a good bass and steady gigs enticed him to join an eighteen-month showband tour of Zululand in the remote South African province of Natal. It was a formative experience for the young bassist, in many ways. "We played schools and hospitals and prisons, and it was very rough," he remembers. "My strings would break and there were no music stores, so I had to patch them and keep playing. My fingers would bleed all over the neck. And since there weren't any supermarkets, either, we ended up not eating much—just living on bread and oranges and sugar cane."

It was on this bare-bones tour that Bakithi made a radical change in his playing technique. "In Zululand I got the dream," he nods. "Before, I was playing everything with my thumb; my uncle's bass player used a pick, so I had never seen anybody play with his fingers. Then I dreamt of somebody playing bass with his fingers, although I couldn't see the person's head. The next morning I woke up and tried to play with *my* fingers. It was a bit difficult, but I worked on it. That dream saved me."

Kumalo's welcome home from Natal was almost as rough as the tour. "My mother could hardly look at me, because I looked so bad from being on the road so long," he recalls ruefully. "She said, 'You have to get a regular job. If you go back to play music one more time, you're not staying in my house!' Luckily, some of my friends called with some recording work. That's when the whole thing started."

Bakithi soon found himself in demand throughout Soweto. "I was really happening," he grins. "I did a lot of local records and got involved in studio work. I was playing twelve songs a day, for about ten rand a track—which is about five dollars [*laughs*]. There were a lot of studios where they liked my playing, but the other bass players really hated me; I was so little and so young, and everybody wanted to work with me. I just wanted to play, and I was really open to learn."

Throughout the '70s and early '80s, Kumalo cemented his reputation as one of South Africa's top session bassists. Along with steady studio work, he often accompanied major international stars on the South African legs of their world tours. Still, he never left his homeland—and he always dreamt of America.

Here Comes Rhymin' Simon

In early 1985, Paul Simon traveled to Johannesburg in search of musicians to help him with his new project—an ambitious fusion of American pop and South African styles that would become *Graceland*. One of the first people he contacted was veteran producer Hendrick Lebone.

"I had done a lot of traditional Sotho music with Hendrick," Bakithi says, "and he knew I was a good bass player. So when Paul said he was looking for musicians, Hendrick called me up. I said, 'Paul Simon? Who's Paul Simon?' [*Laughs.*] So he started to sing 'Mother and Child Reunion' [*Paul Simon*, Warner Bros.] and 'Bridge Over Troubled Water' [Simon and Garfunkel's *Bridge Over Troubled Water*, Columbia]. Aahh, okay, *him*. I knew the songs—but I didn't know who Paul Simon was."

Kumalo and Simon hit it off from their first meeting. "I brought in my fretless, and we started to play some grooves, and it just happened," says Bakithi. "I was tense at first—you know, 'I'm working with Paul Simon, so I'd better knock down these tracks!'—but Paul loved everything I played. Then he said to me, 'I'm going to take you to New York to finish all the tracks.' I said, 'Oh God, yes! Please, it's my dream!' I was really ready to come to the States. I started to listen to British radio for an hour a day to get my English together."

Once in New York, Bakithi gave the rest of the world a taste of Soweto with his work on *Graceland*, and the expatriate bassist found himself exposed to a world of bass playing many of us take for granted. "I heard about Stanley Clarke and Jaco Pastorius," he grins. "And when I first heard Weather Report, I thought, 'Wow, that bass sounds like the bass I'm playing!' [*Laughs.*] Then my ears were really open to everybody playing bass. I listened to Marcus Miller, Victor Bailey—*everybody.*"

After they finished recording *Graceland*, Simon and company embarked on an international tour that was by far the biggest gig Bakithi had ever played. Of course, Paul wasn't the least bit worried. "As a bassist in a live setting," he explains, "Bakithi is extraordinary. He's a very good analyst of rhythm: he lays down a really fundamental groove and he's very solid, but there's always space for the singer."

Kumalo, on the other hand, was terrified. "It was scary!" he blurts. "The first gig we played was in Germany, and I'd never played for so many people. I couldn't face the audience; I just felt like crying. I was praying and meditating before the show: 'Please, I don't want to make mistakes.' And when we played 'You Can Call Me Al,' the people knew the bass solo was coming; I could see they were saying, 'Is this the bass player on the record? We'll find out when that solo comes!' When it was close, they started to watch me. And, man—when I played that solo, I just knocked everybody down! [*Laughs.*] After that, the other shows were like a piece of cake."

It's All in the Fingers

"By the time I played with Paul I was playing the fretless bass," Bakithi says. "I love the fretless; it's a beautiful instrument. It's not at all easy, but you can really make it sing. Growing up in South Africa, I heard traditional singers from a lot of different tribes. Their music is so open, and that's what I try for with my bass playing; I like to hold down the groove, and then I find my space to sing."

Biting the Big Apple

After touring the world with Simon, Kumalo's professional profile grew considerably. He spent several years commuting between Soweto and New York City and, in 1993, committed himself to living in New York year-round. "Friends I met through *Graceland* and the tour introduced me to a lot of people," he says. "And my manager sent out tapes to the jingle houses, just to let people know I was in town. Since then, I've been busy. Will Lee told me, 'Man, people call me and want me to play like Bakithi!' He said, 'Daddy, you'd better take care of business!'"

Since hitting the New York scene, Bakithi has busied himself by backing a host of talented vocalists and instrumentalists, including Cyndi Lauper, Hugh Masakela, Harry Belafonte, Edie Brickell, Laurie Anderson, Gloria Estefan, Randy Brecker, Mickey Hart, Josh Groban, and, of course, Paul Simon. "Just because I'm from South Africa doesn't mean I have to play South African music," he confirms. His five solo CDs also reflect his post-South African influences. "What better place to mix it all together than New York?" says Bakithi. "I hear everything here. Being around so many great musicians is a challenge, but it's great. My dream has come true."

You Can Call Me Al

Three minutes and forty-four seconds into *Graceland*'s sixth cut is a two-bar bass break that has confounded as many bassists as it has inspired. "That was my idea," says Bakithi of the wildly descending lick in the first bar. "We were recording that song on my birthday, and there was a space to fill, so Paul said, 'Go ahead, Bakithi. Do what you like.' I just played—and they *loved* it. It was one take. Listening back, I didn't know what happened; I thought it was from God, you know? I never planned it."

Now for the tricky part: the second bar of the solo is actually the first bar played *backwards*. Engineer Roy Halee simply flipped the tape over and spliced the two parts together. "People have tried to cop those licks," shrugs Simon, "but it's physically impossible." So the next time your band covers "You Can Call Me Al," forget about trying to duplicate Bakithi's mutant solo and take a tip from Paul: Just do what you like.

KUMALO MUSIC

Nothing on *Graceland* exhibits Bakithi Kumalo's "find your space and sing" ethos better than these soaring examples inspired by the title track and "Diamonds on the Soles of Her Shoes." Ex. 1 is in the style of the lilting groove, melodic unison line, and crafty triplet fill Bakithi plays on "Graceland." Ex. 2 recalls the type of lick Bakithi occasionally throws into the verse section of "Diamonds," to augment Simon's buoyant vocal part. It's tricky, especially at tempo and on fretless, but once it's under the hand it'll pour out like melted butter. Don't get bogged down in making the notes only to lose the groove; Kumalo may be outlandishly creative, but never at the expense of feel.

ESSENTIAL GEAR

Fretless Washburn B-40; Joey G fretless four-string and Killer B fretted six-string; Modulus five-string; DR Hi-Beam strings; Aguilar amps.

ESSENTIAL DISCOGRAPHY

Solo albums: *Transmigration*, Guru Project; *This is Me*, Balidali; *Step on the Bass Line*, CCP; *In Front of My Eyes*, Siam; *San Bonan*, Siam. **With Paul Simon** (all on Warner Bros.): *You're the One*, *Rhythm of the Saints*, *Graceland*. **With Herbie Hancock:** *Gershwin's World*, Verve. **With Josh Groban:** *Awake*, Reprise. **With Hugh Masekela:** *Hope*, Triloka. **With Cyndi Lauper:** *Hat Full of Stars*, Epic. **With Gloria Estefan:** *Destiny*, Epic. **With Mickey Hart:** *Spiralingua*, Rykodisc

BILL WYMAN

by Jim Roberts and Greg Isola

Most people know Bill Wyman (born October 24, 1936, in London, England) spent thirty years anchoring the titanic riffs and ramshackle grooves of the Rolling Stones, but few are aware that Wyman's homemade fretless graced a host of early hits by the World's Greatest Rock & Roll Band.

How did you come to the electric bass guitar?

I was trained on clarinet and piano as a child, and I began fooling around with guitar while I was in the Royal Air Force [in 1956]. A few years later [1961, when he was twenty-four], I went to a dance in an old converted cinema. Onstage were the Barron Knights, and the sound of their bass guitar hit me straight on the balls; I couldn't believe the foundation it provided. From that moment, I wanted to play bass.

What was the story behind your first bass, which you converted to fretless?

I was playing in an R&B band in 1961 when I bought a bass from this bloke our drummer knew. It cost me eight pounds [about twenty dollars], and I think it was Japanese. Before that I'd been playing bass on the bottom two strings of a detuned guitar, so I was glad to finally have a "real" bass. Unfortunately, it was bloody horrible! The body was this great big wide thing. But I'd seen Gibson and Fender basses in pictures of Little Richard's and Fats Domino's bands, so I drew a shape like one of those on the back of my bass and had my next-door neighbor saw it down. Then I beveled the edges, took off all the paint, and put in a new Baldwin pickup. Still, it rattled with every note because the frets were so worn. I figured I'd just pull out all the frets and put in new ones when I could afford some. But when I pulled 'em out, it suddenly sounded really good! [*Laughs.*] It had a pure and deep and rich tone. With no frets, you could really slide around on it like a stand-up bass, only you can see where the frets are supposed to be; but you have to be careful because you have to be dead on to be in tune. Anyway, I never put frets back in, and I think it was the first fretless electric ever. I used it on every Stones album and many of the singles up to 1975.

Keith Richards and Charlie Watts are formidable rhythm section mates—but your bass lines really drive "Satisfaction" and a great many other Stones tunes.

"Satisfaction" is a good example: I'm the only one who changes chords. Keith doesn't change, and there are no keyboards on it—there's only me. I just thought walking up to the next chord made it that much better. But when everybody else plays it—Otis Redding did a great cover—they play it on the same chord throughout. And of course the Otis Redding version caused all sorts of trouble because they played the riff in the wrong place, on the root of the chord instead of on the fifth. And the bass just doubled it, staying on the same chord. No one else thought about that

at the time, but for years and years afterward, every time we'd rehearse "Satisfaction" Keith would play it wrong. I used to correct him all the time, and he'd say, "What do you mean I'm fuckin' playin' it wrong—who wrote the song?!" "But you're playin' it like Otis Redding." "Oh, oh, oh, yeah—that's right." [*Laughs.*]

Still, few bands have ever played so well together.

That's because everything we did came from inside. We didn't think about it; we *felt* it. But we are all—Keith, Charlie, and I—quite naive musically. This might amaze you, and it might disappoint a lot of people: if someone says to me, "Go from G up to D♭," I have to think about it because I don't know where the notes are on the bass. Honestly, I don't. I play totally by feel and by ear. So I'd much rather just listen and learn the song than be told, "Go from D to F, then to G for a moment, and then back to the D." I can't think like that, and Keith and Charlie are the same way. If you say to Charlie, "Don't play your bass drum boom-ba *boom*, boom-ba *boom*. Instead play ba-*boom* boom, ba-*boom* boom," he'd say, "That's exactly the same thing!" [*Laughs.*]

How do you explain the Stones' immediate appeal in those early years?

Every other band in England in '63—the Beatles, Gerry and the Pacemakers, the Hollies, Herman's Hermits, the Dave Clark Five, you name 'em—they were all playing [*sings straight-eighth groove*] dut–dut–dut–dut. Every song they played was like that. The Stones were the only band in England—the *only* band—playing shuffle rhythms. We really swung onstage very early on, and it surprised people. Older jazz musicians could do it, but no one expected young kids to play like that—and people just couldn't keep their feet still. Of course when we went to America Jimmy Reed was on all the jukeboxes, especially in Texas—so the shuffle wasn't such a revelation. [*Laughs.*]

Who did you listen to for bass inspiration in those days?

Except for the Chicago stuff with Willie Dixon, most of those records didn't have bass on them. So I tried to find something that fit the music, and I ended up with a style that's quite sparse. I leave lots of holes, because I found the best thing to do on a slow blues is as little as possible. Then when I first heard Booker T. & the MG's in '62, Duck Dunn became my favorite player. I just loved his simplicity; he never got in the way. I knew most people were listening to Keith and Mick and didn't really notice the bass—but that's the way I think it should be.

Bill Wyman Ex. 1

Bill Wyman Ex. 2

I heard all these incredible, magical bass players in those days—Jack Bruce, John Entwistle, John Paul Jones, Felix Pappalardi—but they're all too busy for me. I totally admire their technique; I just can't stand the way they play! It's like another guitar; there's no *underneath*. Ronnie Wood plays like that, too. He'd play on the odd Stones song here or there if I wasn't in the studio, and he'd always ask me later, "What do you think of that, Bill?" And I'd always say, "Bloody horrible! Where's the *bass*?" [*Laughs.*]

You and Charlie didn't play off one another as much as you played together, like one big instrument.

I think I was one of the first bass players in England to understand I had to play along with the bass drum and really concentrate on what Charlie was doing. Jazz people were doin' it, and all the Americans were doin' it—but in England you didn't think like that; you just played along with the tune. I realized very quickly, though, that I should lock in on whatever Charlie was playing on his bass drum, and that's why we fit together so well so early on. The thing is, there was no one to teach you such things. You had to learn by trial and error. Luckily the band learned all these little tricks very quickly.

How much input did the other Stones have on your bass lines?

Well, Keith runs the band; that's old news. But Mick always had the funniest way of suggesting bass lines. He'd

come up to me during sessions and start making playing motions, like Joe Cocker does when he sings. And he'd say, "Play it like [*sings busy, atonal bass line*]." But he wouldn't sing actual notes, so it was useless! When he'd walk away, I'd turn to Keith and ask, "What should I do?" And he'd mumble, "Play exactly what you played before." So I would, and afterwards Mick would come up and say, "That's better!" [*Laughs.*] Mick's got his greatness in many ways, but sometimes he wasn't quite with us musically.

WYMAN MUSIC

Examples of Bill Wyman's pioneering fretless work lurk among some of the Stones' most famous '60s singles. During the climactic final verse and outro of "Paint It Black," Wyman repeatedly slams beats *two* and *four* with heavy-handed E-string glisses that sounded like nothing else on the radio at the time. Ex. 1 recalls this type of slide. "I was the first electric bassist to play those," Wyman nods. "No one else could play like that, but the Stones quite liked it. When we were finished with 'Paint It Black,' though, the boys thought the bass still needed something a bit more *ballsy*. I suggested Hammond organ pedals but then realized I didn't know how to play 'em! So I laid on the floor and punched the pedals with my fists, like you would a xylophone."

Although he eschews the spotlight and *never* solos,

Wyman has a keen sense of melody and a deft touch, especially on his homemade fretless. "I Got the Blues," the haunting "Sister Morphine" (both from 1971's *Sticky Fingers*), and "Loving Cup" (*Exile on Main St.*, 1972) all feature Bill's one-of-a-kind bass and subtle fretless fills. Ex. 2 is typical of these easy-to-finger, box-shaped licks. Notice how Wyman maintains rhythmic consistency across both bars, and dig that oh-so-subtle half-step slide across beats three and four of bar 2.

ESSENTIAL GEAR

Japanese "homemade" fretless, short-scale Vox and Framus basses; Gibson EB-3; wood and Plexiglas Dan Armstrongs; Fender Mustang; Steinberger L-2; Travis Bean; Vox amps.

ESSENTIAL DISCOGRAPHY

Solo albums: *Struttin' Our Stuff*, Velvel; *Bill Wyman*, A&M; *Stone Alone*, Rolling Stones; *Monkey Grip*, Rolling Stones. **With the Rolling Stones:** *Steel Wheels*, Columbia; *Undercover*, Rolling Stones; *Tattoo You*, Rolling Stones; *Emotional Rescue*, Rolling Stones; *Some Girls*, Rolling Stones; *Goat's Head Soup*, Rolling Stones; *Exile on Main St.*, Rolling Stones; *Sticky Fingers*, Rolling Stones; *Get Yer Ya Ya's Out*, London; *Let It Bleed*, London; *Beggar's Banquet*, London; *Their Satanic Majesties Request*, London; *Between the Buttons*, London; *Aftermath*, London; *December's Children*, London; *Out of Our Heads*, London; *The Rolling Stones Now!*, London; *The Rolling Stones No. 2*, London; *12x5*, London; The Rolling Stones, London. **With Buddy Guy and Junior Wells:** *Drinkin' TNT 'n' Smokin' Dynamite*, Blind Pig. **With Willie and the Poor Boys:** *Willie and the Poor Boys*, Atlantic. **With Howlin' Wolf:** *The London Howlin' Wolf Sessions*, Chess.

MICK KARN

by Chris Jisi, Jim Roberts, James Rotondi, and Karl Coryat

Few if any have pulled as many exotic sounds out of the fretless as Mick Karn (born Anthony Michaelides, on July 24, 1958, on the island of Cyprus, and raised in Lewisham in South London). From his early days in the glam/synth group Japan to his solo career, Karn has kept it fresh and strikingly original.

How do you get into bass and who were your influences?

I started on bassoon and—not being a reader—bluffed my way into the London Schools Symphony Orchestra. After our first performance, my bassoon was stolen, but playing it had a big impact on my later bass playing; it was a bass instrument, but it had moments of real melody—sometimes carrying the main melody in the orchestra. Soon after, I purchased a bass guitar for a few pounds and, with Steve [Jansen], David [Sylvain], Rob [Dean], and Richard [Barbieri], we formed what would become Japan. I was pretty disappointed to be stuck with the bass, actually. I had tried being the keyboardist and that didn't work; I even tried being the vocalist and that didn't work—I didn't have the balls for that. So I got demoted to bass. Stanley Clarke was the first bassist who made a big impression on me, with *School Days* [Epic]—although it made me think, "Why am I bothering?" But it was really hard to find any bass heroes when I was young. I was never a Yes fan, but Richard was; *The Yes Album* [Atlantic] was among the records constantly playing over at his house, so I guess I listened to Chris Squire quite a bit—there's definitely an influence there. I was recently listening to one of my favorite records of all time, Lou Reed's *Berlin* [RCA]—and to my amazement, I realized that the bass player is Jack Bruce. I was listening to this incredible-sounding, very slightly fuzzed bass, and I'd never asked myself who it was. Now that I use fuzz bass quite a bit, I guess it harkens back to those days.

How did you get to fretless?

While we were making the second Japan record [*Obscure Alternatives*], I took the frets out of a spare bass at home, and eventually I found it better enabled me to play the melodies I was hearing in my head. So I made the switch and got a fretless Travis Bean. The transition was not easy. At first I definitely had problems with the tuning—especially since the aluminum-neck Travis Bean went out of tune all the time with temperature changes. Rather than hit the note dead-on, I'd move around the note so that at some point in the beat I would be in tune—which might explain my style to this day!

Can you describe your technique and vibrato?

Well, with a violin or cello, you generally get vibrato with wrist movement—but I tend to use my whole arm. In general, I play very, very hard; it's the tip of the finger that touches the string, almost like a claw, rather than the front of the finger. I often hammer with the left hand in a very hard manner up and down the 'board. If you can imagine my hand being like a claw with my thumb hanging over the neck, you realize it's not the normal way you play bass. I usually use just the first two left-hand fingers, and sometimes I clasp my whole hand onto the string and slide up and down the neck, in which case I don't give priority to any one finger. With my left hand, I pluck hard with my first two fingers and occasionally my thumb.

I've never really understood where my ornamentation came from, but with a lot of Near Eastern instruments, like the Greek bouzouki, quite often at the end of a line there's a "whoop" off the string; I guess it must have influenced me without my realizing it. I do the smears because I like the ambiguity of the note. I like to leave a lot up to the listener's imagination; that ranges from concentrating on instrumental music—where the listener has to make up his own theory on what the piece is about—to smearing the notes all over the place so you can't really tell what the root is.

How do you record your bass?

On my solo albums I usually record the bass twice and pan it hard left and hard right so it has a kind of doubled effect. On Japan albums if there were two or three high notes in the part, I would double it the same way just to make it stand out. My philosophy is that most of the tone and sound comes from how the fingers are touching the strings, not by some secret EQ settings. So most basses in most situations can sound fine. Tone-wise, although I like a much bassier, heavier sound, you can lose clarity that way—and harmonics get killed. So I work toward a boosted middle bass. That's what cuts through the best, brings out the harmonics, and gives an unusual tone. A key sonic element on my Wal is the body's tulipwood—they've found only one piece wide enough for a bass. It lends a warmth to the tone that isn't present in my other basses.

How would you describe your bass concept?

Well, I dislike the concept of "lead" bass player. I find a lot of that kind of music self-indulgent and boring. I think of my playing more in vocal terms—providing a key melody while leaving plenty of space for the other instruments. I focus on getting different sounds out of the bass, along the lines of a vocalist singing different vowels. One of my favorite albums is Stevie Wonder's *Songs in the Key of Life* [Motown], which is very heavily vocal. In a lot of black music, the vocal goes places you're not expecting it to—and the rhythms it can come up with are infinite, although it never seems to interfere with the rest of the music. That's not done with instruments very often, but I don't see why. If a voice can do it, why can't a bass? That said, I believe words can't really be trusted; music is a much truer way to express ourselves than words.

KARN MUSIC

One of the highlights of Mick Karn's *The Tooth Mother* is "Gossip's Cup," a hypnotic, churning Mediterranean number in 7/4. Although fairly easy to execute, the bass line is classic Karn—

Mick Karn Ex. 1
♩ = 108

Mick Karn Ex. 2
♩ = 108

Mick Karn Ex. 3
♩ = 108

bizarre, otherworldly, and harmonically enigmatic. There are three parts to the line: the repeating, two-bar A section (Ex. 1), the four-bar bridge, or B section (Ex. 2), and the two-bar C section (Ex. 3), which also repeats. The line's harmonic ambiguity is immediately apparent in section A: after the keyboards establish C minor as the basic tonality, Karn enters on C but within three beats takes it up to C#, and then to D. A neat, sliding major-third double-stop takes the line to the second half of the pattern, where a couple of downward-sliding smears yield to a bouncy, satisfying resolution to C. Mick punctuates the line with his signature swoop up the neck, putting him in position to start the pattern over.

The more harmonically grounded B section (Ex. 2) serves to break up the tune. At the end of bar 1, Karn sustains a G and gives it flavor by sliding it down the neck and back up to where it began. The rest of the bridge consists of long notes and rests that set up the next section.

Just when "Gossip's Cup" starts to make harmonic sense, along comes section C (Ex. 3). This time Karn starts on the major seventh (B), visits C briefly, and ends up at C#, followed by a note that slides around the D string as if searching for a harmonic center. Karn plays this lick with several variations on the record—and sometimes the two doubletracked performances don't agree, leading to momentary low-end chaos. Also of interest are the "blue thirds" within beats three and four, which fall in pitch between E and Eb. The half-flatted E is, of

course, easy to get on fretless, as indicated in the tablature. Bar 2 of the section begins by repeating the first measure—but then Karn uses a trio of curious, offbeat double-stops: a flatted fifth, followed by a fourth, and finally a major third. The progressively thickening texture of these chords enhances the dark, mysterious nature of the tune.

"Gossip's Cup" is straight out of Mick's childhood. "It's a very personal piece—probably the hardest one for people to latch onto," he says. "It was interesting just to home in on the Middle Eastern thing and not let anything else interfere with it. I felt that I was writing almost a traditional Greek song, and I'm really pleased with the way it came out."

ESSENTIAL GEAR
Fretless '81 Wal; Klein K-Bass; DR custom Lo-Riders; Trace Elliot AH600SMX head w/4x10s and 1x15 for larger halls; 2x10/1x15 combo for small gigs; Boss ODB-3 Bass Overdrive pedal.

ESSENTIAL DISCOGRAPHY
Solo Albums: *Love's Glove*, Fullfill L; *Three Part Species*, MK Music; *More Better Distant*, Invisible Hands; *Tooth Mother*, CMP; *Bestial Cluster*, CMP; *Titles*, Blue Plate. **With Japan:** *Tin Drum*, Virgin; *Quiet Life*, Hansa; *Adolescent Sex*, Hansa. **With Kate Bush:** *Sensual World*, Columbia. **With Joan Armatrading:** *Square the Circle*, A&M.

Part 2
Jazz Giants

· · · · · · · · · ·

JACO PASTORIUS

by Chris Jisi, Bill Milkowski, Elton Bradman, and Scott Shiraki

Over the course of his brilliant but tragic life, Jaco Pastorius (born December 1, 1951, in Norristown, Pennsylvania) became synonymous with the fretless bass. In the years since his passing, Bass Player *has covered the father of the fretless well, with in-depth looks at his early years, recordings, bass lines, style, techniques, and gear.*

The Rise of Jaco: 1967–1972

From the moment he burst onto the scene with his incredible solo debut, Jaco revolutionized the electric bass guitar. The uncanny playing on *Jaco Pastorius* [Epic, 1976], with its speed, agility, chordal techniques, improvisational daring, and unprecedented use of harmonics—all delivered with impeccable time and a potent, earthy feel—quickly pushed Jaco to the forefront of the bass world. By 1978, he had attained supernatural status through his virtuosic command of the instrument and his larger-than-life stage presence with Weather Report.

But where did this brilliance come from? How did John Francis Pastorius III become Jaco? To answer those questions, you have to go back to the early years in Fort Lauderdale, Florida, when all of Jaco's influences began to coalesce into the style that changed bass playing forever.

Jaco's first instrument was the drums (his father, Jack, was a drummer), but he switched to bass at age fifteen after breaking his wrist. At the time, he had been playing drums in Las Olas Brass, a local band that played covers of pop hits by the Tijuana Brass, Aretha Franklin, and '60s soul bands. Although Jaco had never touched a bass before, he picked one up at a pawnshop and began playing effortlessly right away, as if he had been predestined to be a bassist. His big hands were definitely an advantage, as were his keen ears and strong sense of time. With these gifts and his innate musicality, it wasn't long before Jaco was creating a stir around South Florida.

Brother Rory remembers Jaco's rapid progress on the instrument: "By the time he was sixteen, he was probably the best bass player in South Florida. By the time he was seventeen, he was definitely the best bass player in the state. Then, just before his eighteenth birthday, Jaco looked me right in the eye and said, really seriously, 'Rory, I'm the best bass player on earth.' I just looked at him and said, 'I know.'"

Brother Gregory contends that Jaco's development was more a product of hard work than divine providence: "We'd be watching TV, and Jaco would practice the entire time, working out patterns on the fingerboard. He had made this mini-amp in shop class at school—he could plug in his bass and a set of headphones—and he'd sit on the couch for hours with that thing, constantly moving his fingers."

Jaco's close friends from Northeast High in Fort Lauderdale, such as drummer Scott Kirkpatrick, guitarist Jim Godwynn, and bassist Bob Bobbing, all recall with amazement how quickly Jaco made the transition from drums to bass. "Within a week," says Bobbing, "Jaco was ripping on the bass. It didn't take long for us to realize he had something special happening." Bobbing was one of Jaco's biggest fans in those days, and is likely the most knowledgeable Pastorius scholar today, with an office full of Jaco artifacts, tapes, and documents.

In assessing Jaco's development, Bobbing cites three important early milestones: "Jaco's metamorphosis from an R&B nightclub bass player to a unique stylist really began in 1967, when he and I walked into the She Lounge in Fort Lauderdale to check out a band. They were called Nemo Spliff, and their bass player, Carlos Garcia, was using a muting technique that was really funky. They played 'I'm Tired,' a Savoy Brown song that was popular at the time, and Jaco really got off on how funky the bass sounded. Carlos had that left-hand muting down and was able to get cool staccato notes happening. Jaco checked that out closely, and then he went home and began experimenting with muting techniques.

"The next thing that happened was harmonics. Jaco already knew about open harmonics, but I'm talking about false harmonics, where you extend your finger and pick behind it. A guy named Clay Cropper showed that technique to me, and I passed it along to Jaco. His initial comment was something like, 'Oh, I've seen guitar players do that. I ain't got time for that. I'm too busy learning this other stuff.' But he eventually picked up on it in a big way.

"The third milestone was when Jaco got his first Acoustic 360 bass amp. Before that, he had been using a Fender Dual Showman, which didn't have much power. Carlos Garcia had a 360, and Jaco got really excited when he heard the sound, so we went down to Modern Music in Fort Lauderdale and bought two of them. With that amp, Jaco had the high end, clarity, and overdrive he needed to *really* rip. He could play chords and project really well. That's what gave him his sound, that amp combined with the sound of his Fender Jazz Bass and the muting technique he picked up from Carlos Garcia. A little later, he started using Rotosound strings, which gave him a brighter sound and longer notes, and he really got his voice together on the instrument."

Several of Jaco's intimates from the early years point to the organ trio Woodchuck as a key element in Jaco's evolution. "That was a killer band!" recalls Scott Kirkpatrick. "They had Jaco on bass, Bob Herzog on drums, and a guy on Hammond B-3 named Billy Burke who was like the Jimmy Smith of South Florida. They had a house gig at Code One in Fort Lauderdale, and all the musicians in town used to drop by there to check them out."

Bobbing was equally excited about Woodchuck. "That was the band that really put Jaco on the map in South Florida," he says. "They had so much feeling and soul. Las Olas Brass was nothing special, just a Top 40 cover band, but Woodchuck was *it*. That's where Jaco's Jerry Jemmott funk lines started coming together, and that's when he started to become a performer. He was singing, and he had a lot of charisma onstage. It was the greatest little band in the world."

In 1970, Jaco hooked up with an R&B group called Tommy Strand and the Upper Hand. Kirkpatrick, who played drums in the band, recalls Jaco as "the ultimate groove player" even back then. "We had the house gig at the Seven Seas Lounge on Collins Avenue in Miami Beach," he recalls. "I tell you, I've *never* played with anybody since who could groove like Jaco. I don't think there ever will be anybody else with that kind of groove power. He was so funky, and it wasn't that thumb-slap thing that's happening today. I don't think Jaco ever got into that stuff. He was playing with two fingers and laying down the funkiest, most innovative lines I've ever heard in my life."

Around that time, Jaco began to supplement his income by working on the cruise ships that sailed from the Port of Miami. The music was cocktail-lounge jazz standards, but when the ships docked in places like St. Thomas and Nassau, Jaco went ashore to mingle with the local calypso and reggae musicians. He added the Caribbean sounds to his vocabulary, and their influence can be heard readily in the music he made with Weather Report and with his Word of Mouth big band.

During the summer of '70, Jaco married his high school sweetheart, Tracy Lee Sexton. On December 9, 1970, Tracy gave birth to a daughter, Mary. Jaco took the responsibility of fatherhood quite seriously and became determined to make it as a musician in order to support his new family. "I remember when Mary was born," says Gregory. "We were in the hospital looking at her through the glass in the maternity ward, and Jaco said, 'Well, Greg, this is it. Now I gotta be the greatest bass player that ever hit the planet. There's this little baby here now, and I gotta make a real living at this and not just play in stupid bars all my life.' He was ready to take on the world."

Early in 1972, Jaco joined Wayne Cochran and the C.C. Riders. "He was playing an hour and a half nonstop, three sets a night, five nights a week or more," says Bobbing. "It was a big horn band with no keyboard, so Jaco was able

to experiment with chords, harmonics, and that soloistic approach he became famous for, all while laying down an incredible groove. Every time the band would break it down, Jaco would be right there cooking, doing all his cool funk turnarounds. That gig was like the oven for Jaco Pastorius."

Charlie Brent, guitarist and musical director of the C.C. Riders, recalls Jaco's audition: "I was looking to replace a guy who was leaving, and someone recommended this kid named Jaco. We went to see him at a place called Marco Polo in North Miami, where he was playing with Tommy Strand and the Upper Hand. I was completely floored by what I heard, so I asked Jaco to come up to Bachelors III in Fort Lauderdale, where we were playing that week. He showed up one afternoon, and I whipped the book in front of him and counted off the show. He just completely burned it to pieces! He wasn't a great reader, but he told me he had caught the show a couple of weeks before and remembered the music!

On the road with the C.C. Riders, Brent would sit in the back of the bus with Jaco and quiz the young bassist about the circle of fifths and other bits of music theory. "It was a rough grind," says Allyn Robinson, former drummer with the C.C. Riders. "We would do forty one-nighters in a row: work our way from Chicago down to Miami, spend two weeks in Miami, and then hit the bus again and work our way up the East Coast, over to Chicago, and back down to Miami. But every time I saw him, whether it was on the bus or at the hotel, he'd have a bass in his hands. The guy was so motivated, it was inspiring."

On the gig, Brent relied on Jaco's inimitable grooves to drive his charts, and he often stood in awe of the sheer chops and ingenuity he heard on the bandstand. "He always played too much shit, which made everybody else crazy, but his time was so meticulous that it never got in the way of anything that I wrote," says Brent. "He had perfect meter from the day I met him. There were times when Wayne would send the horns out into the audience and leave us up there vamping for fifteen or twenty minutes. Just Jaco, Allyn Robinson, and me, playing 'Cleanup Woman' while all the horns were down the street with Cochran, who was climbing a telephone pole. I mean, it was a wild band, you know? And Pastorius would cover both the rhythm guitar and bass parts at the same time while I took solos. That's when he got into playing changes with harmonics, just to fill in while we were up there vamping.

"I remember when he started playing fretless. We were

somewhere in the Midwest, and Jaco said, 'Man, I wanna try one of those fretless basses.' So he goes down to the hardware store and buys some alligator pliers and wood compound. He takes those pliers and goes at the bass, tearing all the frets out—I mean, wood was flying. I was going crazy, yelling, 'Don't do this. That's the only axe you got on the road. You ain't gonna be able to play the gig tonight!' But I swear, that night he played better than he ever played. He was doing slides and all the other things he couldn't do on the fretted. I guess he had been thinking about how he'd play a fretless, but he had never really screwed around with it before. It was fucking amazing.

"One time when we were in Texas, he started hitting the harmonics on the first, second, and third frets—doing changes down there at the bottom. I'd never heard anybody do anything like that, but he had such a *touch*. He'd hit different strings with different pressure, do different changes—he could get three different chords at the second fret. When he started doing that stuff, that's when I knew he was the messiah, man." Continues Brent, "I taught Jaco everything I knew about music; all about chord voicings and arranging, and then I left him running the band. If it wasn't for his personality, he might still be running that band. But he only lasted a few weeks after I left. He didn't have me to run interference for him, and Wayne just didn't want to put up with him anymore."

Today, both Brent and Robinson look back at Jaco's ten months in the C.C. Riders as a special time in their lives. "It was just magic," says Robinson. "I haven't had anything like that since. The most beautiful thing about Jaco's playing wasn't the obvious stuff like playing fast and all that. It was his phrasing. He knew when to play and when not to play—a lot of times, he would just lay out. The music dictated the way he played, and he always made it say something. Jaco was always true to the style, and anything he put on top of it seemed to fit like it belonged there. He was very groove-conscious, and he loved that backbeat. No matter how much facility he had, he loved to groove more than anything else."

"There'll never be another," concludes Robinson. "There's bass before Jaco and there's bass after Jaco. That's just the way it is. His playing was so emotional and so creative. And it wasn't cluttered—busy as his stuff was, it always flowed. It was like a living, breathing thing; it had that yin and yang. That was the beauty of his playing, and that's what people miss. I mean, this guy was touched by God. There's no way you can duplicate him. All you can do is get a little bit of what he was all about and try to develop on that, try to complement his concept. Let the door that he opened open up doors for you."

On the twentieth anniversary of his tragic death, *Bass Player* paid homage by peeling away the layers of a Pastorius classic.

Jaco's Finest Hour: Weather Report's "Havona"

"Come here and take a look at this." The request came from legendary engineer Ron Malo, whose recordings at Chess, Motown, Capitol, and other labels ranged from Chuck Berry and Muddy Waters to the Rolling Stones and Billy Joel. He was speaking to young engineer Brian Risner. On the other side of the glass, an equally youthful Jaco Pastorius had just plugged in for his Weather Report audition track: "Cannon Ball," from the album *Black Market*. As Risner relates, "Ron said, 'All I have is maybe 3dB of peak limiting and almost no EQ, and it's not even going into limiting. There's only one other bass player I've ever worked with who got this great a sound from his hands, and that was James Jamerson.'"

To mark the twentieth anniversary of the tragic death of the bass guitar's most formidable figure, John Francis Pastorius III (on September 21, 1987, from a nightclub beating, in his native Florida), in a positive light, we've decided to analyze an all-time Jaco classic (with commentary and analysis from Jimmy Haslip, Christian McBride, Steve Bailey, and Janek Gwizdala). So cue up the track and follow along.

A Song Is Born

Among Jaco's bass anthems, when it comes to the triple-threat combination of composition, bass line, and solo, none stands quite as tall as "Havona." Pastorius originally wrote the tune in late 1973, while under the spiritual influence of *The Urantia Book*. A chapter in the book describes "Havona" as the master galaxy (which contains Earth)—and as a perfect universe consisting of a billion spheres of unimagined beauty. A raw version featuring Herbie Hancock, Lenny White, and Don Alias was recorded for Jaco's 1976 landmark solo debut, but it was not included. When Sony re-released *Jaco Pastorius* in 2000, with bonus tracks, the decision was made not to include "Havona," sparking a controversy among fans.

The preeminent "Havona" version came a year later, for Weather Report's 1977 epic, *Heavy Weather*. Strikingly fresh and uninhibited, the track dances and soars on an ear-grabbing bass line, partnered with a sizzling drum groove. Meanwhile, angular changes provide fodder for the consensus baddest bass guitar solo ever put to tape. As drummer Alex Acuña told Joe Zawinul biographer Brian Glasser, "I think my favorite [track on *Heavy Weather*] is 'Havona.' That, for me, is how I always want to play, that kind of a conversation. When I hear that tune, I still get the chills. Everything was improvised in that moment—it's almost no overdubs." Perhaps Peter Erskine, who succeeded Acuña in Weather Report, sums it up best. "As the final track on *Heavy Weather*, it's one of those tunes on one of those albums that, when you've finished listening to it, you want to listen to the entire recording from the beginning all over again. It is a perfect track and is one of my all-time favorite Jaco performances. Oddly, it was one of the few tunes that the band did not rehearse or try to play live when I was in the group, but I'm grateful for its existence. 'Havona' is definitive Jaco: incredible rhythm, new and fresh harmony, virtuosity—flawless execution and intonation, including his Stravinsky quote!—and a sense that the song is coming from the past and the future at the same time."

Studio Meteorology

Brian Risner, who engineered *Heavy Weather* with Malo, and did live sound for Weather Report from 1972 to 1983, summons up some details of the session. "It was late 1976, and we were at our usual spot, Devonshire Sound Studios, in North Hollywood. The room there is like a live echo chamber, which is why there's so much 'air' in Weather Report recordings. There was no need for tight miking or much miking in general, with the room supplying all that ambience and an open, accurate, spatial sound." Jaco played his '62 Jazz "Bass of Doom," with its fretless rosewood neck and new Rotosound roundwounds. Risner recalls that while Jaco's Acoustic 360 rig was miked against the upper grille with an Electro-Voice RE-20, that was only twenty-five percent of the sound; the other seventy-five percent was his direct signal through a stock M.C.I. board, with a "drop" of limiting in a few spots, via a Universal Audio 1176.

Jaco, Zawinul, Shorter, and Acuña recorded the song live (percussionist Manolo Badrena didn't play on the track). Explains Risner, "Jaco brought the piece in new, so they were all reading it; I remember it was the most chal-lenging song on the album. They ran it down a few times, and in those days a reel of tape was fifteen minutes, so you'd play the tune twice in a row for each take. I can't recall how the bass solo was done, but there were at least three tracks of bass available, so Jaco could have edited it together from different passes. I just remember that Jaco, Joe, and Wayne were always present, for anyone's overdubs or punches."

Havona: Six Minutes of Sublime Sub-Hook

"Havona" begins with Zawinul's seemingly random synth-chord stabs, locked in when Acuña's cymbal-led kit enters. Synth and kit roll on, building the suspense that's capped by Acuña's superb two-bar cymbal break. At last, Jaco's bass bursts forth with such deftness and presence it's hard to focus on Shorter and Zawinul's tied-whole-note melody. Immediately, Jaco establishes his use of all the chord tones available: sixths, major sevenths, and seconds/ninths are as prevalent as roots, fifths, and thirds. Notes Christian McBride, who recorded the tune on upright for his CD *Sci-Fi*, "It's ingenious the way his note choices switch between being melodic and serving as the bass function. His first notes are a great example; he delays the root on the downbeat by first playing the second and sixth. It shouldn't work on paper, but no matter how many times I perform the tune, I've got to play the bass line that way—it's part of the song. Strong-beat/weak-beat is simply not an obstacle for him! That gives credence to the bass line being as much of a melody as, or counter-melody to, his sparse written melody."

Janek Gwizdala agrees: "In a way, Jaco is soloing throughout the song. He's not sticking to an ostinato bass line; he's developing motifs that are so melodic you could make new compositions out of most of them." In fact, the two-bar length of most of the changes seems designed to allow Jaco to fill or complete his phrase in the second measure. Steve Bailey best puts it in perspective. "An interesting aspect is how Zawinul and Wayne Shorter let Jaco dominate the music and the mix; their solos are softer and panned to the sides, while the bass is hot throughout. Essentially, the track is just a bass line and a bass solo, with some accompaniment. It's almost not about the bass fitting the music—it's about the music fitting the bass."

As the first head finishes up, we arrive at what Jimmy Haslip calls "the torturous turnaround lick." McBride marvels, "How do you even get it in your brain to want to play that? It's like jumping off a building and then saying, 'Now I want to jump back up!'" Steve Bailey agrees: "The first time I heard that lick I freaked out; later, when I got to know Jaco in Florida, I asked him to show it to me, and I remember he had two different fingerings he used to play it." McBride offers, "There's no chord change played, but it implies a C Lydian scale starting on the seventh (B); actually, knowing Jaco's piano side, it almost sounds like it could be the arpeggio of a chord voicing he came up with."

Speaking of chord changes, it's worth noting the basic pattern of major chords moving in major thirds (E–C/B–G). Is this perhaps influenced by the kind of chord movement Coltrane used in "Giant Steps," which Jaco would later cover on *Word of Mouth*? Also, one can't help but contrast Jaco's "Teentown," with its dominant seven (thirteen) chords moving in minor thirds. Suggests Gwizdala, "You can point to earlier tunes like Joe Henderson's "Inner Urge" (1964), with the same kind of movement; music schools call it 'parallel constant-structure chords'—a chord progression consisting of three or more chords of the same quality. But I think this was just Jaco finding his own voice."

Keyboardist/arranger Gil Goldstein, who worked with Jaco and his music, offers, "There was a sense of 'correctness' in Jaco's voice leading. That was a word he used a lot, and he made sure his chords and solos fit into that mold. I remember seeing him swiftly and accurately playing voicings at the piano with his wide reach and pinpoint aim. Referring to 'Havona' specifically, there are parallel structures, but what made it interesting was the relationship of the outer voices: the top note of the voicing to the bass note. That was where Jaco created the magical tension that propelled his voice leading and made them sound so mysterious. I believe he learned this from Gil Evans, who was Jaco's inspiration in many ways. Similar to 'Havona' in this interesting relationship between the outer voices are the voicings in 'John and Mary' [from *Word of Mouth*, Warner Bros.]. Of course, good contrary motion is not something new—every music student hears about it in counterpoint class or harmony lessons—but few come to be able to control those elements in a musical and personal way, and Jaco's use of that idea was magnificent and totally his own."

Joe and Wayne's World

Zawinul's potent piano solo and Shorter's snaking soprano sax solo follow the head, respectively. For Zawinul's turn, Jaco breaks it down via perfectly intonated fifths. Says Gwizdala, "Making those fifths work against such dense

chords reminds us that his touch was phenomenal; it's what changed modern electric bass playing." Jaco starts percolating again, leading McBride to note, "You can clearly hear Acuña's brilliance here, with his hip hybrid of swing and Latin, reminiscent of Airto with the first edition of Return to Forever. Alex and Jaco came into the band together and really had the hookup." A true Jaco highlight occurs at 1:33. "Those two measures are sequential melodic genius," says Bailey. "And the twist is, he starts with dominant seventh-to-root for the Em chord, but instead of changing it to major-seventh-to-root for the E major chord, he goes with sixth-to-major-seventh!" Gwizdala adds, "It's brilliant, but it's a lick; notice that it reappears later. Jaco likely figured out that one on the Wayne Cochran tour bus four years earlier. But that's cool; look at Michael Brecker, a self-confessed lick player. All the greats play licks, but they have them so together they're able to incorporate them fluidly in a variety of appropriate settings."

Following another "torturous turnaround" run, Wayne Shorter begins blowing. Jaco breaks it down again, this time with perfectly intonated octaves of the roots and thirds of the chords. As the pace picks up, Gwizadala points out, "So much of the band's comping is Q&A stuff all the way through. As with any great band, they listen more than they play."

Solo of Doom

Jaco's historic solo arrives at 2:34. Haslip, who recorded the tune in 2003 with the Word of Mouth Big Band, sets us up. "My jaw dropped when I first heard Jaco's awesome solo; what hit me next was how well balanced it was: technique, lyricism, flow, and heart—essential ingredients for music that will stand the test of time. I spoke to Jaco soon after, and he told me the solo was a composite of three passes, but where the edits are I don't know." Jimmy continues, "The opening motif is killer, as memorable as John Williams's motif from *Close Encounters of the Third Kind*. For the answering phrase, with its C Lydian flavor, I always hear 'Maria,' from Leonard Bernstein's *West Side Story*. The next quote is from Igor Stravinsky's *Rite of Spring* intro."

As Jaco gets more linear, coming out of the gorgeous motif at 2:47, our panel offers speculative harmonic analysis. Haslip: "To my ear, I hear E minor with chromatic passing tones; E Lydian; A minor; C Lydian; A♭ minor pentatonic; and B minor pentatonic." Gwizdala: "One of Jaco's favorite devices was to play the minor pentatonic a half-step below a major seven chord. So if he had a Cmaj7, playing a

B minor pentatonic scale—B, D, E, F♯, A—would touch in all the upper-extension color tones—major seventh, ninth, tenth, and sharp eleventh. He also liked minor pentatonic scales a minor third down from the root of a major 7 chord; and here, against the Bmaj6/9(♯11) chord, you can call that A♭ minor pentatonic or even A♭ Dorian, because he gets the sixth in there, the E♯/F♮." McBride sums up the linear content more directly: "It's bebop, man; it's a bionic version of Bird. He's thinking like a horn or piano. At that time, few if any had played like this on electric or upright bass. Guys were soloing over II–V's, but to be exploring the upper partials of altered and poly-chords in these kinds of progressions was unheard of."

Way Out of the Box
Jaco begins his second chorus with a more involved (though no less melodic) statement that continues into the first half of the next measure. More so than in his first chorus, he builds overall momentum and intensity by playing extended lines between his melodic stopping points. Gwizdala observes, "The rhythmic displacement, where he plays descending groupings of four, six, three, and five sixteenth-notes, is classic Jaco; it's reminiscent of the groups of four notes he plays against triplets in 'Donna Lee,' or the five-against-four groupings in his 'Continuum' solo."

McBride puts the solo's closing extended phrase into perspective. "If we had met a medium in 1975 who said in the next year there's a bass player who is going to play those nine measures, we would have thought they were delusional! It's just an insane passage up and down the fingerboard, and it's likely one long idea, with no punches. Best of all, it gets badder as it goes along, setting up the consummate climax, with Jaco touching on all the chord tones while bouncing off the open G string." Gwizdala points out, "That closing figure reminds us of how Jaco was into wide intervallic leaps, which give your lines a very horn-like sound. If you recall on his instructional video/DVD [*Jaco Pastorius: Modern Electric Bass,* Warner Bros.], in addition to scales and arpeggios, Jaco stressed working on all kinds of string-jumping intervals." He concludes, "Jaco's creativity behind this solo was *way* out of the box."

Back to the Head?
A return to the head is portended following the bass solo, with Zawinul playing the melody on synth an octave down from the original head, loosely doubled by Shorter. But

soon, Zawinul is also playing a full-blown right-hand piano solo that continues up to the turnaround lick. On the bottom, Jaco has some more dazzling moves to come. Bailey digs how Jaco finishes his two-bar groove phrase, with no root to be found in the first bar, and no fear of playing the flat five on the downbeat of the second. McBride likes the fresh rhythmic idea that follows, almost a half-time swing approach. Next, Jaco lets loose with a gorgeous upper-register fill (using the ninth, sixth, and tenth). Says Gwizdala, "Jaco loved songs and singers, from Sinatra to Aretha to Broadway, so he knew the sweet notes." In contrast, as if finally boiling over with sonic adrenaline, Jaco then unleashes a torrent of trills.

The next section also begins undefined. Instead of stating the melody again, Shorter fills, while Jaco resonates on fifths before introducing the track's first harmonics. Both finally get back to the melody, doubling it to dramatic effect—Bailey's favorite moment in the track.

Outrageous Outro
An extended outro on the B7sus pedal begins next. At first, Shorter whoops and wails, while Jaco plays edgy syncopations between his low As and Bs. His four sixteenth-note B's seem to catch Zawinul's ear. As Bailey notes, Zawinul takes the idea and turns it into steady-sixteenth Bs on piano for an entire bar; Jaco catches this and begins doing it himself. Says Steve, "When Jaco begins looping the Bs, check out how he shades them with varying dynamics." McBride adds, "His time on the Bs is so dead-on; it reminds me of what he later did with steady As on 'Port of Entry' [from Weather Report's Night Passage]." As Jaco comes out of the pattern, Zawinul restates the intro chords (while Shorter makes a sly reference to the steady Bs in two different octaves). Jaco bides his time, leaving the bottom to Zawinul's synths and grabbing just the last three melody notes. Overtones from an unknown source ring subtly from the last chord, giving the listener a good ten seconds to absorb the sonic spectacle that has just occurred.

Have At It
"'Havona' is indeed a glorious piece of music," marvels Bailey. "Victor Wooten has always maintained that Jaco was able to play as busily as he wanted because he grooved so darn hard and with such intensity. As a result, my advice, when attempting to play it, is to focus on the time and groove first and foremost. Then the part will begin to flow." Haslip adds,

"Ultimately, for both the bass line and solo, it's about understanding the harmony as thoroughly as Jaco did, and exploring it for yourself." Gwizdala takes it a step further: "You really should transcribe the bass part if you're going to learn it. Make sure you listen to it closely until you can sing the entire part and solo without your bass in your hands. This way the music will get deep inside of you. And be ready to forget about it as soon as you've learned it all. The less time it spends in the forefront of your mind, the less it will cloud your own personal voice on your instrument. That's the goal, because that's what Jaco had above all else."

JACO TOOL KIT

"Havona" has many but not all of Jaco's trademark fingerboard moves; here's a list of the main ones.

1) Sustain and Vibrato: Jaco's singing fretless tone is instantly recognizable and especially poignant on melodies like "Continuum" and Weather Report's "A Remark You Made." There are several keys to achieving his trademark slow attack/slow decay notes. To start with, while Jaco slid, hammered, pulled off, and trilled into notes, when he wanted to be especially expressive he'd often use a three-finger roll. Target a note you want to play with your third finger, but first play the note two frets below with your index finger, then quickly hammer your middle finger on the next fret and then your third finger on the target note; this all-in-one motion will create a slight delay, adding impact to the note. Next, Jaco favored a classical-string-player-like, side-to-side vibrato; while sitting on the target note, use a subtle side-to-side motion with your finger, hand, and even your arm (keeping your thumb anchored behind the neck), while also rolling your finger pad on the note. Pause slightly to establish the pitch before adding vibrato, like a vocalist does, so the note will sound more natural. Also key is your plucking hand placement; striking the strings with a lighter attack just below the fingerboard will provide your notes with maximum swell.

2) Natural and False Harmonics: Having practically invented the use of extensive harmonics for explosive, sonically cutting melodies and chords on the bass guitar, Jaco was a master of both natural and false or artificial harmonics. His landmark "Portrait of Tracy" is a thesis on natural harmonics; Weather Report's "Birdland" is no doubt his most famous false-harmonic line; while "Amerika" incorporates both. Natural harmonics are basically about touch and geography. Once you've identified key harmonics at various dividing points—called nodes—over the string's length (such as the twelfth, seventh, fifth, and fourth frets), touch the string over the fret with your index finger, without pressing down. Then pluck the string, removing your index finger an instant later, sounding the bell-like tone of the harmonic. Playing harmonics on multiple strings led Jaco to the discovery of some interesting chords.

False or artificial harmonics work on the same principal of dividing the string between wherever your fretted note is and the bridge. For example, if you're fretting an E♭, on the eighth fret, G string, go to the halfway point (the twentieth fret) and place your index finger over that fret. Next, reach behind your index finger with your thumb and pluck the string, releasing your index finger an instant later. An E♭ harmonic should sound. You can also reverse your fingers, using your thumb as the "capo" and your index finger to pluck the string, which was Jaco's preferred method.

3) R&B Staccato Sixteenths: Like Rocco Prestia and Jerry Jemmott (who Jaco used to sneak into Criteria Studios in Miami to hear) before him, Jaco was a master of the busy-but-seamless groove. To duplicate his stuttering sound, favor your bridge pickup, move your plucking hand back by the bridge, and play short notes with the tips of your index and middle fingers. Use the alternate finger as well as your fretting hand to help deaden the plucked notes. To perfect your feel and sense of how to interchange pitches and ghost-notes to the fullest groove effect, checkout Jaco's "Come On, Come Over," "The Chicken," and Herbie Hancock's "4 A.M." On the Latin side, go with Jaco's "Used to Be a Cha-Cha," "Invitation," and, of course, "Havona."

4) The Jaco "Two-Feel": On the swing side, one of the numerous ways Jaco modernized his instrument was to come up with a funky alternative to walking (though he could stride with the best of them). Jaco's bounce—playing half-notes and catching the last triplet of beats two, four, or even one and three—added rhythmic punch and drive, while giving way to the occasional walked measure or two. To hone your own two-feel, be sure you know your chord tones and listen to Jaco's "Liberty City" and Joni Mitchell's *Mingus* album, a virtual textbook on the approach, from bright tempo ("Dry Cleaner from Des Moines") to ballad ("Goodbye Pork Pie Hat").

PASTORIUS MUSIC

Bass Player excerpted or completely transcribed many of the Jaco classics found in the Hal Leonard transcription series.

One of the bass lines examined that has not been included in any Pastorius books to date was Jaco's riveting swing-meets-funk groove on Joni Mitchell's "The Dry Cleaner from Des Moines," from her 1979 collaboration with Charles Mingus, *Mingus*. The following examples typify some of Jaco's moves on the track. Ex. 1 is in the style of his climbing intro figure, in which he plays the third, seventh, and ninth of the dominant ninth chords. In Ex. 2, Jaco's use of the third and the sixth as bouncing points becomes a signature theme throughout the song's tonic chords. Jaco also liberally uses and implies jazz substitutions, as shown in measure 4, which works over the tritone substitution (E7♯11 for B♭7) leading to the IV chord. Finally, Ex. 3 is similar to a bebop-borne turnaround lick that Jaco plays, which he later incorporates into his horn arrangement on the track, played twice as fast. Be sure to check out the live version of the song from Mitchell's 1980 disc, *Shadows and Light*, for more Jaco magic.

ESSENTIAL GEAR

Although Jaco was known to say his tone was "in his hands," the gear he chose was an important component of the "Jaco sound" and image. At a time when most bassists sounded like variations of James Jamerson or Larry Graham, Jaco's sweet and punchy pre-'65 Fender Jazz Basses (with the bridge pickup wide open and the neck pickup backed off to varying degrees), bright Rotosound Swing Bass RS66 roundwound strings, and warm Acoustic 360 amp helped him fuse the upright's vocal-like, expressive qualities and the electric's quick and defined attack. Jaco settled on this combination by 1972 and largely stuck with it until his death in 1987.

Jaco claimed to have owned over a hundred basses in his lifetime. Most were early-'60s Jazz Basses with the pickguard and pickup covers removed and the stack-knobs replaced with the three-knob configuration. Here's a look at some key pieces in the Pastorius palette, with insights and comments from two people who knew Jaco's gear best: Bob Bobbing, who met Jaco in early '68, and Florida repairman Kevin Kaufman, who worked on Jaco's basses beginning in '78.

1967 Fender Jazz, serial no. unavailable

Fifteen-year-old Jaco got his first electric bass, a new sunburst Fender Jazz with binding and pearl blocks, in 1967. He strung it with La Bella flatwounds and played it through a Sunn amp in Las Olas Brass, and with the organ trio Woodchuck. It was his main electric until 1971.

1962 Fender Jazz, a.k.a. the "Bass of Doom," SN 57308

Like the fate of a mythic hero's mighty weapon, the original condition and final resting place of the world's most famous fretless were shrouded in mystery until recently (see below). Its legendary tone was well documented through every era of Jaco's career, and he himself told several versions of the tale.

According to Bill Milkowski's August '84 *Guitar Player* cover story, the '62 Jazz was already fretless when Jaco bought it in Florida for $90. Upon meeting Kaufman in 1978, Jaco told him he had removed the frets himself with a butter knife and filled in the slots and missing fingerboard chunks with Plastic Wood, followed by several brushed-on coats of Petite's Poly-Poxy. Kaufman's first job for Jaco was to replace the peeling epoxy, which he did by using his own method of pouring on the epoxy in one treatment and shaping it with a rasp.

Kevin recalls a huge repair job he did in the mid-'80s after Jaco had apparently smashed the Bass of Doom in an argument. Kaufman and fellow repairman Jim Hamilton painstakingly glued together what remained of the '62—fifteen large chunks and several small pieces (the hardware and electronics were still functional.) They inlaid wood where fragments were missing, laminated a figured-maple veneer on the front and back, and repaired the shattered headstock by laminating an ebony/maple veneer to hold it together. Refinished in a two-tone sunburst, it was returned to Jaco in New York. Kevin says it still sounded great.

According to Kaufman, Jaco left it in New York's Central Park shortly before his death. In 2006, it was brought in and sold to a New York City guitar shop. The current owner, who has made the bass available to other New York City pros and members of the Pastorius family, is still contemplating the instrument's fate.

1960 Fender Jazz, SN 64437

Jaco's main fretted Jazz Bass, a two-tone sunburst, of average weight and "very resonant" according to Kaufman. This was Jaco's main bass on tour with Joni Mitchell; it can be seen and heard on her *Shadows and Light* album and DVD. Its whereabouts are unknown.

Acoustic 360 and Effects

The Acoustic 360 amp, which debuted in 1968, featured a 200-watt power amp. The separate preamp had a built-in fuzz

Jaco Pastorius Ex. 1

♩ = 184

Bright halftime swing

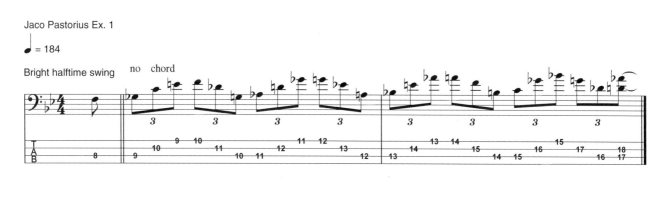

Jaco Pastorius Ex. 2

♩ = 184

Bright halftime swing

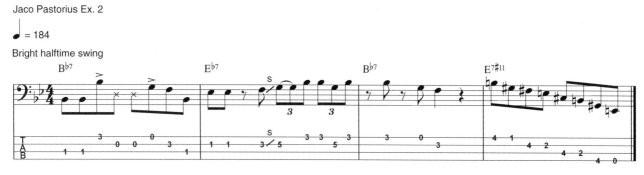

Jaco Pastorius Ex. 3

♩ = 184

Bright halftime swing

effect, and the large cabinet housed an 18" backward-firing speaker. Jaco almost always played through two 360s. In 1984, Jaco told *Guitar Player*, "I usually put the bass setting all the way up and the treble about halfway up, depending on the condition of the strings. The older the strings, the more treble you have to have." SWR founder and current Raven Labs head Steve Rabe serviced Jaco's amps in the '70s while working for Acoustic. He notes, "They weren't modified at all; I just made sure they were in top-notch shape. I didn't say much to him—I'd just listen and watch him play. I noticed he played way back by the bridge. The 360's frequency response has a bump centered at about 200Hz, and I often wondered if part of his right-hand location was to compensate for that bump."

As for effects, Jaco at times employed the built-in fuzztone on his Acoustic 360, an early MXR Digital Delay through his second 360 rig for a chorus/flange effect without loss of bottom, and an Electro-Harmonix sixteen-second digital delay to create groove loops to play against (as on Weather Report's "Slang" and Jaco's "Giant Steps/Reza").

ESSENTIAL DISCOGRAPHY

Solo Albums: *Portrait of Jaco: The Early Years*, Holiday Park; *Modern Electric Bass* [Instructional DVD/Video], DCI; *The Birthday Concert*, Warner Bros.; *Invitation*, Warner Bros.; *Word of Mouth*, Warner Bros.; *Jaco Pastorius*, Epic. **With Weather Report** (all on Columbia): *Weather Report*; *Night Passage*; *8:30*; *Mr. Gone*; *Heavy Weather*, Black Market. **With Joni Mitchell** (all on Asylum): *Shadows and Light*; *Mingus*; *Don Juan's Reckless Daughter*, *Hejira*. **With Pat Metheny:** *Bright Size Life*, ECM. **With Herbie Hancock:** *Mr. Hands*, Columbia. **With Flora Purim:** *Everyday Everynight*, Warner Bros. **With Michel Colombier:** *Michel Colombier*, Chrysalis.

RUSH ON DVD BRAZILIAN RHYTHMS YELLOWJACKETS RISE AGAINST

BASS PLAYER®

A MUSIC PLAYER PUBLICATION | AUGUST 2006

WWW.BASSPLAYER.COM

DIG DEEPER

MUSIC!
ARETHA FRANKLIN
'ROCK STEADY'
CHUCK RAINEY'S
COMPLETE BASS LINE

HOG WILD!
LES CLAYPOOL
GOES (MORE) NUTS WITH
NEW ALBUM, NOVEL & FILM

MASTERING
COLTRANE CHANGES

ISRAEL & NEW BREED
FUNK FOR GOD'S SAKE

ERIC CLAPTON'S
'AFTER MIDNIGHT'

7 GEAR REVIEWS
TWO-PICKUP STINGRAY
NS DESIGN BASS CELLO
LINE 6 LOWDOWN COMBOS
BODY GLOVE GIG BAG
AND MORE!

$5.99 U.S. $7.99 CAN.

08>

CMP

0 09281 01012 8

BASS®
PLAYER

A MUSIC PLAYER PUBLICATION | NOVEMBER 2006

WWW.BASSPLAYER.COM

DIG DEEPER

MUSIC!
SUBLIME
'WRONG WAY'
COMPLETE BASS LINE

LEARN TO PLAY
MILES DAVIS
'SO WHAT'

THE
HIPPEST
EVER?
PINO
PALLADINO
WITH **THE WHO**
& **JOHN MAYER TRIO**

EDGAR MEYER
ULTRA-HARD
MASTER CLASS!

8 GEAR REVIEWS
NEW EPIFANI RIG
RETRO-COOL SQUIER BASSES
PHIL JONES BASS SUITCASE
DINGWALL FANNED-FRET J BASS

HOW TO PLAY
BRAZILIAN
FUNK

$5.99 U.S. $7.99 CAN.

0 09281 01012 8

11>

POWERMAN 5000 STUDIO SECRETS
BLUES TRAVELER'S NEW GROOVES

BASS
YER

SUGAR RAY

Gospel Great
ANDREW GOUCHÉ

NATHAN EAST
With
Eric Clapton

JACK BRUCE
CUTS LOOSE!

SEPTEMBER 2001

$4.95 U.S. , CAN. $5.95, U.K. £3.25

0 9>

0 71486 01012 8

A MUSIC PLAYER PUBLICATION

NEW IMPROVED PRODUCT REVIEWS!
NEW G&L 4-STRING
TRIPPY NEW BOSS PEDALS & MORE

BASS PLAYER ™

MUSIC!

RIGHTEOUS REGGAE ROCK

RAY BROWN JAZZ SOLO

UNEARTHED JACO LESSON + MORE

JACO
Evolution OF A
Genius

23 TOP BASSISTS GO DEEP
FOR ALLEN WOODY

Flea, Claypool, Bootsy, MeShell, Entwistle ...

JANUARY 2002

$4.95 U.S., CAN. $5.95, U.K. £3.25

A MUSIC PLAYER PUBLICATION

Versatile MXR D.I.+
Funk-Filled EBS Head
Slick Brian Moore 5-String
Innovative Upright Pickup

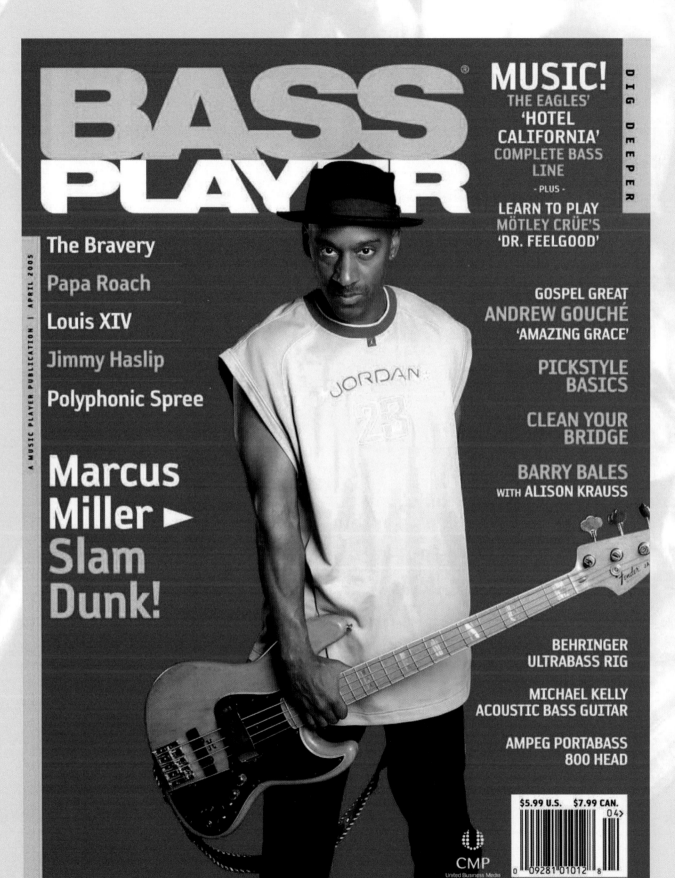

BASS PLAYER®

PLAYER

A MUSIC PLAYER PUBLICATION | APRIL 2005

DIG DEEPER

MUSIC!
THE EAGLES'
'HOTEL
CALIFORNIA'
COMPLETE BASS
LINE
- PLUS -
**LEARN TO PLAY
MÖTLEY CRÜE'S
'DR. FEELGOOD'**

The Bravery

Papa Roach

Louis XIV

Jimmy Haslip

Polyphonic Spree

Marcus Miller ►
Slam
Dunk!

GOSPEL GREAT
ANDREW GOUCHÉ
'AMAZING GRACE'

**PICKSTYLE
BASICS**

**CLEAN YOUR
BRIDGE**

BARRY BALES
WITH **ALISON KRAUSS**

**BEHRINGER
ULTRABASS RIG**

**MICHAEL KELLY
ACOUSTIC BASS GUITAR**

**AMPEG PORTABASS
800 HEAD**

$5.99 U.S. $7.99 CAN.
04›

0 09281 01012 8

CMP
United Business Media

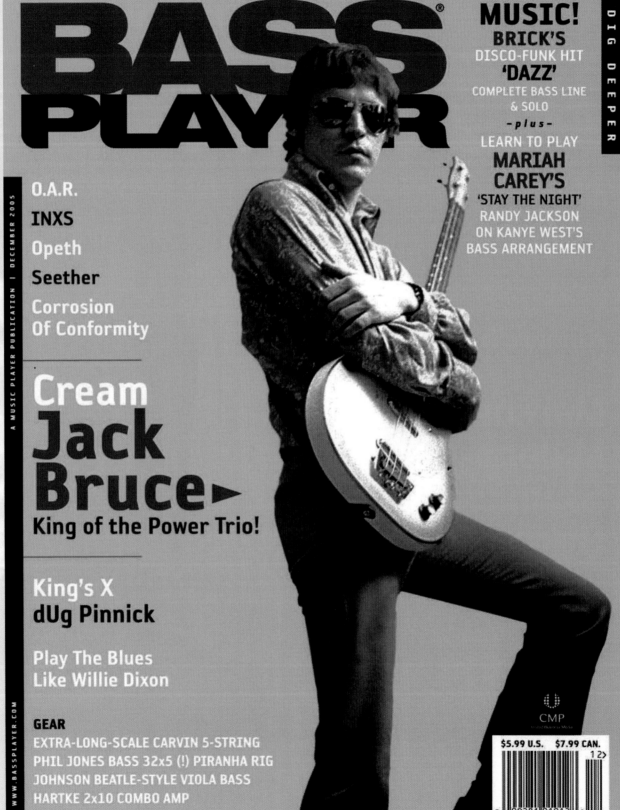

BASS PLAYER

A MUSIC PLAYER PUBLICATION | DECEMBER 2005

WWW.BASSPLAYER.COM

DIG DEEPER

MUSIC!
BRICK'S
DISCO-FUNK HIT
'DAZZ'
COMPLETE BASS LINE
& SOLO
– plus –
LEARN TO PLAY
**MARIAH
CAREY'S**
'STAY THE NIGHT'
RANDY JACKSON
ON KANYE WEST'S
BASS ARRANGEMENT

O.A.R.
INXS
Opeth
Seether
Corrosion
Of Conformity

Cream
Jack
Bruce ▶
King of the Power Trio!

King's X
dUg Pinnick

**Play The Blues
Like Willie Dixon**

GEAR
EXTRA-LONG-SCALE CARVIN 5-STRING
PHIL JONES BASS 32x5 (!) PIRANHA RIG
JOHNSON BEATLE-STYLE VIOLA BASS
HARTKE 2x10 COMBO AMP

CMP
United Business Media

$5.99 U.S. $7.99 CAN.

12>

0 09281 01012 8

BASS
PLAYER

NEW CD!

See Page 66

MICK KARN
CUTTING-EDGE FRETLESS

CHRISTIAN McBRIDE

ANDY WEST

Reviewed
TRACE ELLIOT TUBE AMP

JANUARY 1996
DISPLAY UNTIL JAN 1

$3.95 U.S., CAN. $4.95, U.K. £2.75

THE WORLD'S **#1** BASS PUBLICATION

7 70989 35577 4

A MILLER FREEMAN PUBLICATION

NEW COLUMN!
DAVID
ELLEFSON
OF MEGADETH

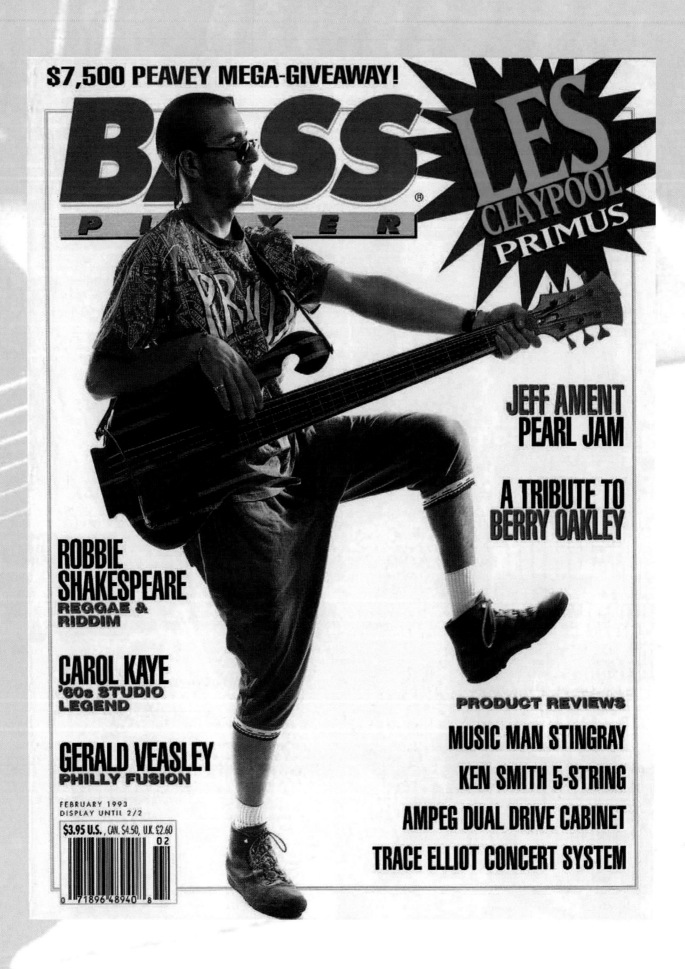

$7,500 PEAVEY MEGA-GIVEAWAY!

BASS
PLAYER

LES
CLAYPOOL
PRIMUS

JEFF AMENT
PEARL JAM

A TRIBUTE TO
BERRY OAKLEY

ROBBIE
SHAKESPEARE
REGGAE &
RIDDIM

CAROL KAYE
'60s STUDIO
LEGEND

GERALD VEASLEY
PHILLY FUSION

PRODUCT REVIEWS

MUSIC MAN STINGRAY

KEN SMITH 5-STRING

AMPEG DUAL DRIVE CABINET

TRACE ELLIOT CONCERT SYSTEM

FEBRUARY 1993
DISPLAY UNTIL 2/2

$3.95 U.S., CAN. $4.50, U.K. £2.60
02

0 71896 48940 8

BASS PLAYER

A MUSIC PLAYER PUBLICATION | SEPTEMBER 2007

WWW.BASSPLAYER.COM

DIG DEEPER

MUSIC!

THE DOOBIE BROTHERS
'LISTEN TO THE MUSIC'

MARCUS MILLER WITH LUTHER VANDROSS
'NEVER TOO MUCH'

ELVIS COSTELLO & THE ATTRACTIONS
'PUMP IT UP'

20 YEARS AFTER

JACO
DECONSTRUCTING 'HAVONA'
HIS GREATEST BASS PERFORMANCE

LEE ROCKER
A STRAY CAT'S NEW STRUT

JONAS HELLBORG
TONE ZEALOT

DOOBIE BROTHERS
TIRAN PORTER

SHRUNKEN HEADS!
3 POWERFUL BASS AMPS UNDER 5 POUNDS
EA iAMP MICRO-300 ▪ MARKBASS F1 ▪ EDEN WTX-260
PLUS! NEW ESP BASSES
SEYMOUR DUNCAN PARANORMAL BASS DI

HOW TO *REALLY* LOCK WITH THE DRUMS
PAGE 90

$5.99 U.S. $7.99 CAN.

0 09281 01012 8   09>

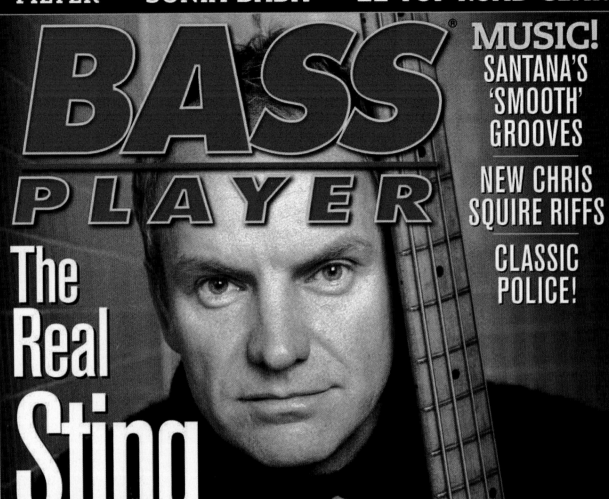

FILTER • SONIA DADA • ZZ TOP ROAD GEAR

BASS® PLAYER

MUSIC!
SANTANA'S 'SMOOTH' GROOVES
NEW CHRIS SQUIRE RIFFS
CLASSIC POLICE!

The Real Sting

How He Writes Songs
What He Practices
Why He Loves Bass

MARCH 2000
$4.95 U.S., CAN. $5.95, U.K. £3.25

0 71486 01012 8   09>

A MILLER FREEMAN PUBLICATION

GEAR REVIEW BLOWOUT!
BASSBALLS UPDATE • NEW DIGITAL AMP
BARGAIN HI-END 5-STRING & LOTS MORE!

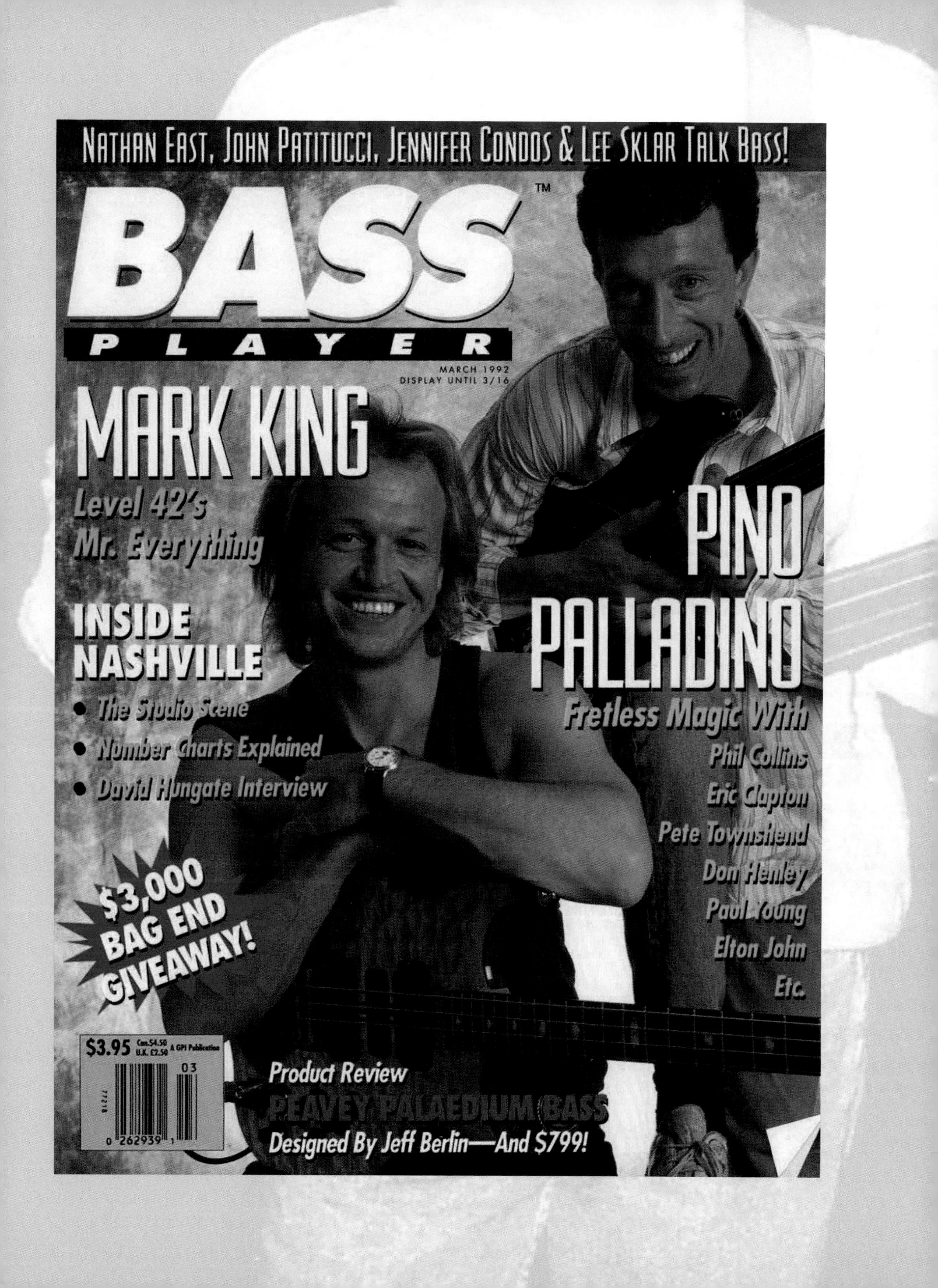

NATHAN EAST, JOHN PATITUCCI, JENNIFER CONDOS & LEE SKLAR TALK BASS!

BASS ™
PLAYER

MARCH 1992
DISPLAY UNTIL 3/16

MARK KING
Level 42's
Mr. Everything

INSIDE NASHVILLE

- *The Studio Scene*
- *Number Charts Explained*
- *David Hungate Interview*

PINO PALLADINO
Fretless Magic With

Phil Collins
Eric Clapton
Pete Townshend
Don Henley
Paul Young
Elton John
Etc.

$3,000 BAG END GIVEAWAY!

$3.95 Can.$4.50 U.K. £2.50 A GPI Publication

03

7 72218

0 262939 1

Product Review
PEAVEY PALAEDIUM BASS
Designed By Jeff Berlin—And $799!

Vintage Basses: *What They're Worth & How To Restore Them*

Elvis Lives!

BASS™
PLAYER

APRIL 1992   DISPLAY UNTIL 5/4

STING
Exclusive Interview

Stage Gear

Best Bass Lines

Complete Transcription With Tablature:
"Every Little Thing She Does Is Magic"

Making It As A Pro
A Clinic With Jeff Berlin

Alphonso Johnson
A Bass Clinic With Jeff Berlin

Reviewed:
Tobias Standard Bass
Gallien-Krueger Amp
Yamaha Multi-Effects

Win Phil Lesh's $3,600 Modulus Graphite 6-String!

$3.95 Can.$4.50 U.K. £2.50

01

0 262939 1

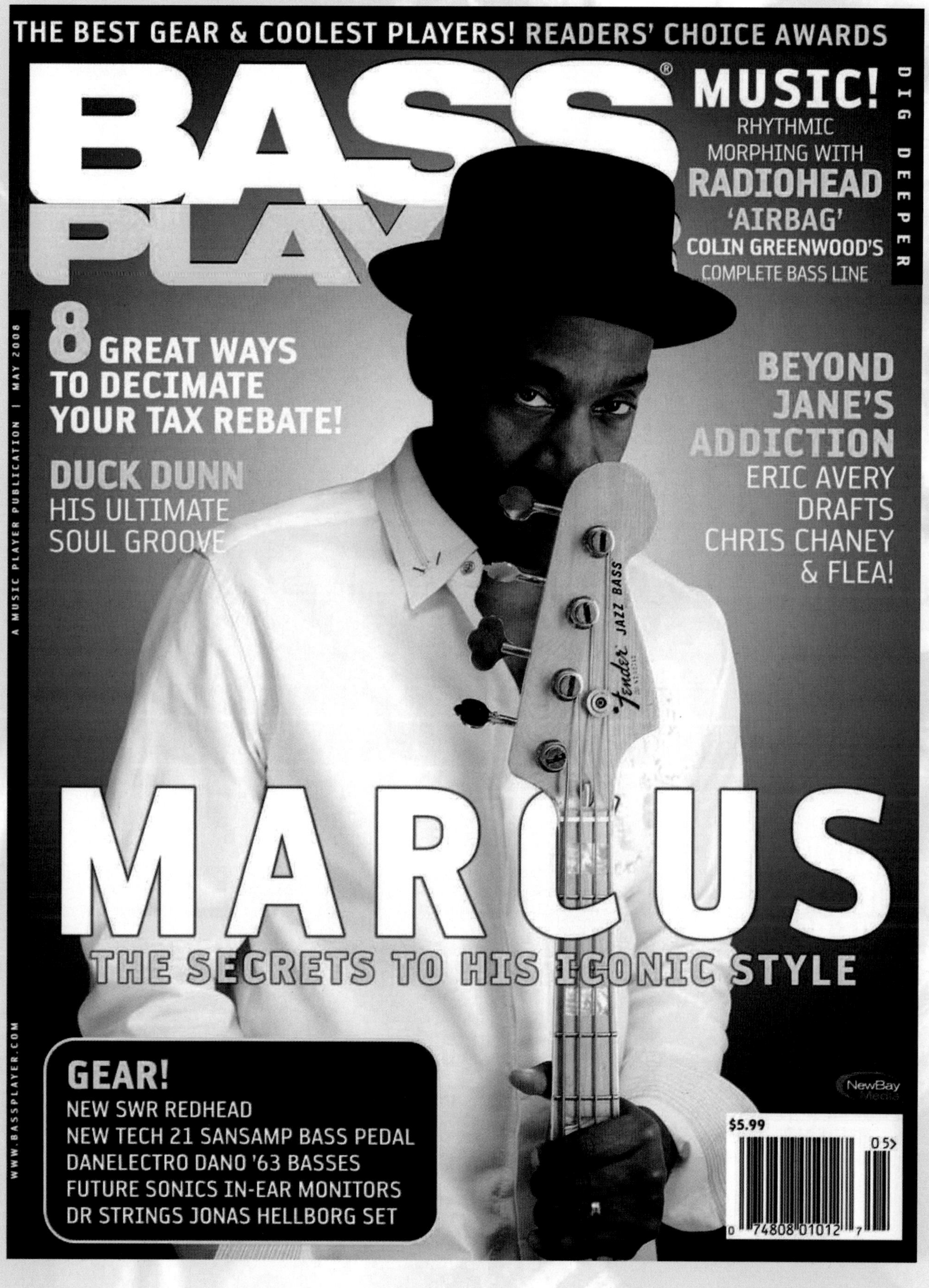

THE BEST GEAR & COOLEST PLAYERS! READERS' CHOICE AWARDS
BASS PLAYER®
DIG DEEPER
MUSIC!
RHYTHMIC MORPHING WITH
RADIOHEAD
'AIRBAG'
COLIN GREENWOOD'S
COMPLETE BASS LINE
A MUSIC PLAYER PUBLICATION | MAY 2008
8 GREAT WAYS TO DECIMATE YOUR TAX REBATE!
DUCK DUNN
HIS ULTIMATE SOUL GROOVE
BEYOND JANE'S ADDICTION
ERIC AVERY DRAFTS CHRIS CHANEY & FLEA!
Fender JAZZ BASS
MARCUS
THE SECRETS TO HIS ICONIC STYLE
WWW.BASSPLAYER.COM
GEAR!
NEW SWR REDHEAD
NEW TECH 21 SANSAMP BASS PEDAL
DANELECTRO DANO '63 BASSES
FUTURE SONICS IN-EAR MONITORS
DR STRINGS JONAS HELLBORG SET
NewBay Media
$5.99
05>
0 74808 01012 7

BASS
PLAY

NEW!
SWR
6X10
KILLER
CAB

ALAIN CARON
FUSION LIVES!

T.M. STEVENS
FUNK+ROCK=
BOOM!

EXCLUSIVE
REVIEW
THE BEST
UPRIGHT BASS
TRANSDUCERS

JUNE 1996

$4.50 U.S., CAN. $5.50, U.K. £2.75

0 70992 3557 8

A MILLER FREEMAN PUBLICATION

WIN!
CURBOW + EDEN
$12,500
GIVEAWAY

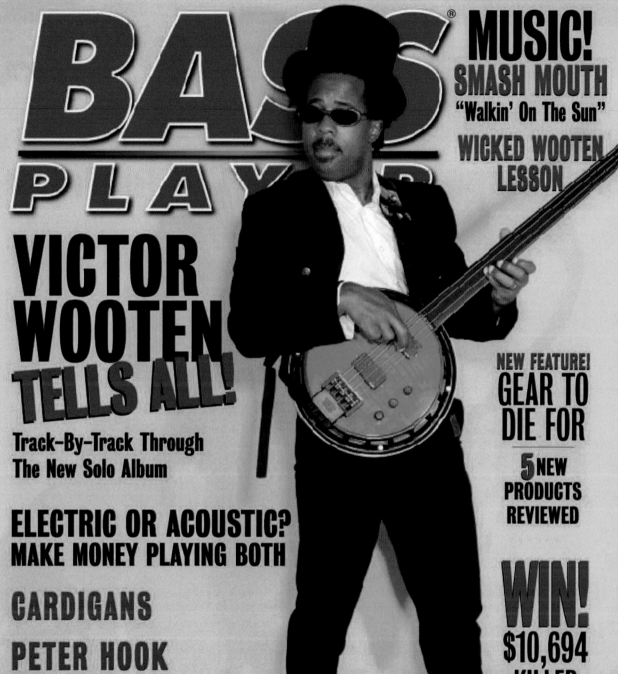

BASS PLAYER

MUSIC!
SMASH MOUTH
"Walkin' On The Sun"

WICKED WOOTEN LESSON

VICTOR WOOTEN TELLS ALL!

Track-By-Track Through
The New Solo Album

ELECTRIC OR ACOUSTIC?
MAKE MONEY PLAYING BOTH

CARDIGANS

PETER HOOK
Still A Punk?

NEW FEATURE!
GEAR TO DIE FOR

5 NEW
PRODUCTS
REVIEWED

WIN!
$10,694
KILLER
BASS RIG
Giveaway

FEBRUARY 1998

$4.95 U.S. , CAN. $5.95, U.K. £2.75

A MILLER FREEMAN PUBLICATION

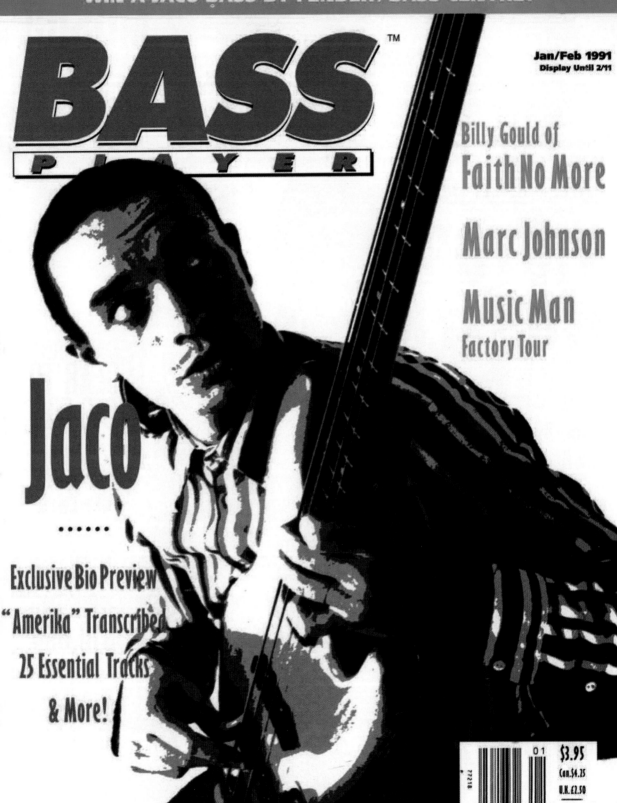

BASS
P L A Y E R ™

Jan/Feb 1991
Display Until 2/11

Billy Gould of
Faith No More

Marc Johnson

Music Man
Factory Tour

Jaco
......

Exclusive Bio Preview
"Amerika" Transcribed
25 Essential Tracks
& More!

$3.95
Can.$4.25
U.K. £2.50

0 262939 1

01

A GPI Publication

GARY WILLIS

by Chris Jisi, Bill Leigh, Ed Friedland, and Anil Prasad

More than just a state-of-the-art fretless monster, Gary Willis (born March 28, 1957, in Longview, Texas) has raised the bar in the art of improvised grooves and solos, as well as the technical/educational aspect of bass playing, with his right- and left-hand methodology and light-touch approach.

The most exciting aspect of your playing is your ability to blur the line between soloing and groove playing.

That's due to the influence of jazz, where the rhythm section has a responsibility to listen and respond—to go places with the soloist. It makes the music more interesting to listen to, so we try to include that in all of our tunes. There are certain set sections and parts, but a lot of the solo sections are not as specified, so we can develop the groove as the soloist develops his solo. Consequently, the music takes on different forms from night to night.

How does that affect the bass/drums relationship?

It opens things up. You're still responsible for time-keeping and for creating a "locked" feel with the drummer, but if you latch onto certain figures, especially with the kick drum, it can be a problem if one of you changes. So you have to focus on the whole kit and develop your instincts to get an intuitive sense of where you should play together and where you're free to try ideas.

The foundation for a lot of your improvisational grooves is the 16th-note pulse made popular by two of your influences: Jaco Pastorius and Rocco Prestia.

They're the inspiration, sure, along with Paul Jackson. But it's something I worked on after hearing bassists who were technically limited to playing eighth-notes get left behind when the soloist and drummer kicked the energy up a notch by playing sixteenths. I wanted to be in control enough to hear and execute ideas in that pulse, so I could participate and make things happen. The most important element is the use of ghost notes; they provide the illusion of space and the accents that really propel the groove. If I played a pitch on every note, the bass lines would be far too busy.

In your instructional focus on right-hand technique, you talk about using three fingers and playing with a light touch.

Most bassists learn music through their left hands, with their right hands sort of tagging along. By addressing the right hand independently, you can gain the kind of control that will eventually help you to develop a style. Using a three-finger technique allows me to play things that wouldn't normally occur with just two fingers.

As far as using a light touch goes, once I got good equipment I started playing softer and got a better sound. Playing a note softly will result in the same attack as playing a note hard, but the tone will be fatter. Plus, you have more range and control of dynamics when you play with a light touch. For me, that's most effective when I'm grooving because I have to move a lot of air on the dead notes to feel the accents.

How did your light right-hand touch come about?

From not ever having a bass teacher and having to discover techniques myself, as well as from my early frustration playing too hard due to crappy amps and loud drummers. I took a "physics for musicians" class in college and learned that if you pluck a string softly and crank the amp, it produces the same attack as a string plucked hard—but the tone is fatter for the duration of the note.

When you play a groove or a solo, even at high volumes, a lot of the feel is determined by your dynamics. By training yourself to use a lighter touch at all intensity levels you're still able to vary your dynamics when everything is cranking. Another factor is that on fretless there's a fine point to attacking the string so it will sing, which is why I need a volume pedal to back off some notes at very low stage volumes.

Even though you play fretless, you tend to stay away from slides and heavy vibrato. Why?

Sliding is easy and available on the fretless, but I don't hear it, personally, because it's not something you do naturally with your voice. The same is true of exaggerated, nervous-sounding vibrato. Coming from playing barre chords as a guitarist, I worked on getting my first finger where I wanted it and where it was in tune. That meant spending two years with my head bent forward, eyeing the fingerboard. But eventually you learn the neck of your bass and develop muscle memory.

A good way to work on intonation is to record a drone note and play against it, making it any part of the harmony—the root, the third, the ninth. Then play different scales around it. That helps you to get into the habit of relating everything you play to something else.

To me, fretless intonation is hand-eye coordination. The first thing I'd recommend is fretlines. And always practice with a pitch. The next big advantage you can develop is the ability to be mobile, to roll your finger and make minor adjustments. In addition to having a musical vibrato, I'm adjusting the pitch. A fretless note should never be static.

You've inspired a lot of players to use palm muting. How did you develop that?

I stumbled on it in the '80s while trying to play reggae grooves in various bands. At first I put my palm on the strings and used a pick, but I quickly abandoned that and used my fingers instead. I've incorporated it more and more over time for a number of reasons: it sounds bigger and moves more air, and it fits better underneath guitar and keyboards. I can also maintain high levels of energy and note activity without getting in the way. Musically I like the control it gives; as the intensity picks up I can gradually back off into regular tones or sometimes start individual notes muted and remove the palm pressure, letting them swell into full-blown notes.

What are the keys to creating a lengthy bass solo that's interesting both to you and the listener?

First of all, you have to have something to say. You have to tell a story through your solo and make it evolve over time. The musical context, composition, and groove all have to work together to justify the solo. I favor melodic ideas that are fully developed and followed, and that effectively contrast with the piece's other components. Coming up with a great bass solo is like writing a part for a character in a movie, because a movie is only as good as what happens to its characters. So, if the initial soloing idea isn't allowed to evolve, and it gets discarded or isn't fully acknowledged by its surrounding environment, the listener will likely lose interest.

Is that idea related to your overall philosophy as a bassist?

Definitely. It's really important to take responsibility for what you do on your bass by creating interesting surroundings to justify its existence. It's one thing to be able to say things on your instrument, but if you don't create your own opportunities, you are totally dependent on being a sideman in someone's vision of where your playing fits. You might find a sideman gig with someone whose musical vision is totally aligned with yours, but the odds of that happening are really slim. Also, in order to have something to say, you need to have a life outside of music that motivates you to express something unique. If you only devote your time to the instrument and practicing, there won't be any drama or humanity in your playing.

Your main bass is your signature fretless Ibanez five-string; how has the instrument evolved since it debuted in 1999?

At this point in its development, it's pretty much perfect for me. It's a bolt-on bass with light ash, which provides a focused attack but still resonates low frequencies very well. It also has a minimal finish with just a sanding sealer, because the more finish and paint you apply to a body, the less open and more compressed the sound is. The bass use is a custom Bartolini humbucker, and the coils are designed

and carefully positioned to deliver a warmer sound on the higher strings and a fat, clear, deep sound overall. The pickup is integrated with a ramp I've developed that sits under the strings; it's designed to eliminate the possibility of grabbing too much string and playing too hard. It also provides a place for your thumb. You adjust the pickup and ramp height with a single tool that's provided with the bass.

In 2002, you published the book *101 Bass Tips*. Do you have any new tips to offer?

The element of physics is one I didn't include. It seems like a contradiction, but if you're playing in a small rehearsal room, you need more power and amplification than in a big concert hall. I've found that I'll be at a certain volume in a small studio, and then I'll get on a big stage and have to turn down the volume. It has to do with the fact that you need large walls to really reflect low frequencies. So, realize that your need to project may be the opposite of what you expect. Also, keep in mind that your sense of time is tightly controlled by what happens with your plucking hand. If you want to be a clean and efficient player, your fretting hand has to be imperceptibly early. Some people just intuit that and get it, but others have to dig in and teach their left hand to take care of business before a note gets played. It's a real puzzle for some people who haven't developed that sense; they'll think their sense of time is messed up or their ability to play fast is affected by something they just can't figure out, when it's really all about this one issue.

WILLIS MUSIC

Gary Willis is in peak improvisational form throughout his solo CD, *Actual Fiction*, as his ever-evolving fingerboard ideas transition effortlessly between gnawing grooves and linear melodic motifs rife with tension and release. Example 1 contains four measures of Gary's solo on "PodCast," at 4:13. His bass is doubled by two Melodyne plug-ins of B-3 organs, creating a harmonized effect. Says Gary, "I was tempted to get a horn player for the solo because I wanted long, weaving lines with chromaticism, so that's the approach I took." Check out how he employs a three-note chromatic figure that always ends on a chord tone some eleven times during the example—most impressively in bars 2 and 3, where he rhythmically displaces them.

Example 2 shows five bars of Gary's singing fretless solo on "Say Never," at 2:08. For negotiating the chord movement of major chords a whole step apart, Gary offers that he played over D minor for the B♭ and C chords, and D major for the

Gary Willis Ex. 1

♩ = 148

Bright funk

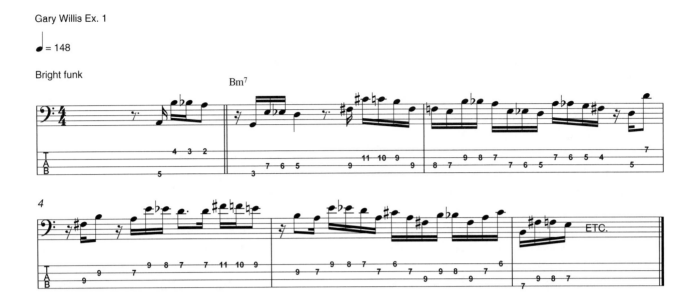

D chord. He also handles the tricky rhythmic placement of the chords nicely, especially with the tasty motif he develops in the last two measures. Lastly, Example 3 features Gary's percussive, percolating groove solo at 2:42 of "Eye Candy." He allows, "My goal in improvising, whether it's a groove or a solo, is to express ideas in a conversational way. I try to create energy, and one of the best ways to do that is with intervals. This section revolves around the repeated E♭s and Cs, and the way they're varied, displaced, and augmented with other notes and intervals."

ESSENTIAL GEAR

Ibanez Gary Willis Signature GWB1005 fretless five-string; custom Ibanez ATK305 fretted five-string;

D'Addario XL165s; Aguilar DB 750 amp with three Aguilar GS 112 1x12 cabinets; Lexicon MPX1 multi-effect; T.C. Electronic G-Force multi-effect; Roland V-Bass.

ESSENTIAL DISCOGRAPHY

Solo albums: *Actual Fiction*, Abstract Logix; *Bent*, Alchemy; *No Sweat*, Alchemy. **With Slaughterhouse 3:** *Slaughterhouse 3*, Abstract Logix. **With Tribal Tech:** *Rocket Science*, Tone Center; *Thick*, Zebra; *Illicit*, Bluemoon; *Tribal Tech*, Relativity; *Nomad*, Relativity; *Dr. Hee*, Passport; *Spears*, Passport. **With Wayne Shorter:** *Phantom Navigator*, Columbia. **With Allan Holdsworth:** *None Too Soon*, Restless; *Metal Fatigue*, Enigma. **With Scott Kinsey:** *Kinesthetics*, Abstract Logix.

Gary Willis Ex. 2

♩ = 82

Legato ballad

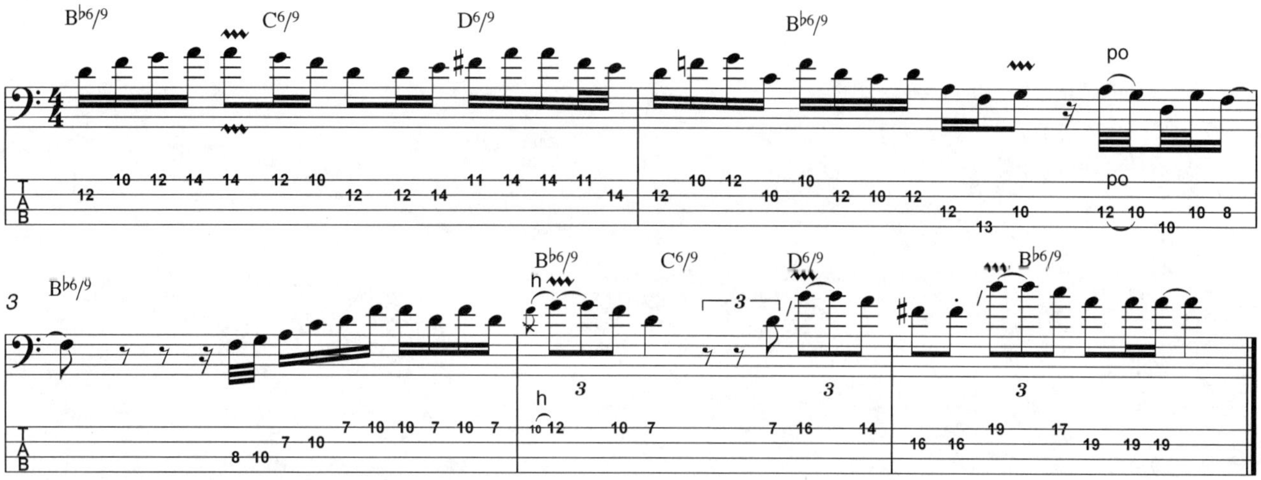

Gary Willis Ex. 2

♩ = 132

Bright staccato funk

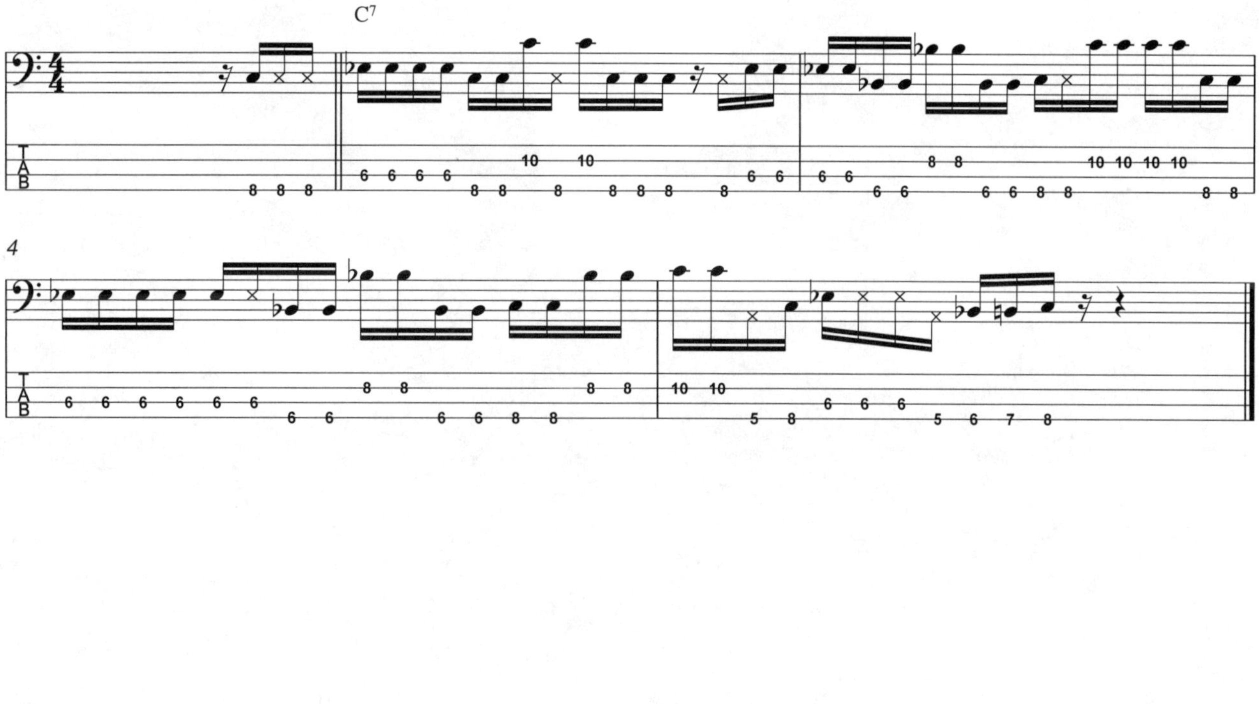

MARK EGAN

by Jim Roberts and Chris Jisi

Mark Egan (born January 14, 1951, in Brockton, Massachusetts) is one of the cornerstone voices of the fretless bass, inspiring a whole school of imitators on the instrument's smooth, melodic side. His coveted career ranges from solo artist with his own label to in-demand New York session ace.

Your solo on Pat Metheny's "Jaco" is a classic; where did you develop your melodic solo style?

By then I had located and was refining my own voice. But the search and development of that voice began on trumpet, which I played from the time I was ten until I was in college. As a teenager, I became interested in jazz after hearing Chet Baker. His extremely melodic and expressive style had a big influence on me. At the same time, I was into pop music of the time. I was first attracted to bass because of James Jamerson's prominently mixed parts on Motown records, which were a fixture on the radio. By the time I switched to bass, in my second semester at the University of Miami, I had an understanding of its function as well as knowledge of improvisation and melodies, from playing trumpet. I quickly realized the bass guitar had a rich, almost cello-like tone which gave it a voice of its own; I remember playing a friend's fretless Precision and thinking it had great possibilities—it combined the warmth of an acoustic bass, which I also played, with the sustain and clarity of the electric bass.

When I joined Pat Metheny, Jaco gave me my first fretless, a '58 P-Bass he had gotten from Pat and converted. I tried it and it worked with Pat's music, so I ended up using it almost the whole time I was in the band.

Where do you get the inspiration for tunes on your solo CDs?

Most of my compositions come from things I discover on the bass, a fragment of a melody or a particular pattern. I'll work on that for a while, maybe jot something down on paper, and then I'll develop it more fully on computer. In addition, I like to create a balance between composition and improvisation; I like to create backdrops for myself—sometimes with a live-playing situation, other times with layering. As for outside influences, I really love Indian music, especially the droning aspect; I find it mesmerizing. I also listen to a lot of classical music, especially Bartók, Ravel, Debussy, Stravinsky, and Messiaen. And I'm always going back to the other "classics," too: Jimi Hendrix, Charlie Parker, Miles Davis, John Coltrane—people like that.

Intonation is one of the most difficult aspects of fretless, yet you multi-track with fretlesses. How do you keep them in tune?

All of my Pedulla fretless basses have inlays where the frets should be, and I keep my eye on the markers and keep my ears open. I also spend a lot of time getting the doubled parts right and tuning up between tracks. I use an electron-

ic tuner, and I'm a real perfectionist. I like to get it right because I hate to hear records where something is out of tune. I got a lot of my pitch awareness from playing trumpet, because when you're in a horn section, you must be in tune. If you aren't, you get thrown out. Playing scales on string bass with a bow alongside pianists helped me, too.

Do your basses have especially low action?

Yes. It allows me to get that buzz and long sustain.

Working in the studio as much as you do must help your intonation.

The studio is like a mirror. When you put something down on tape and you play it back, sometimes it's very revealing. Using you ears is a craft that you gradually develop. I'm always working on it. It's a constant struggle on fretless bass because your ears and fingers must constantly adjust. And if the bridge isn't set right when you put your finger down at the fret line, you're out of tune. Every time you change strings, you should check the bridge's intonation in relation to the harmonics. My instruments' setup is very critical. For example, season changes can have an effect. This past fall, it got very dry, and all my necks started to bow, making the strings higher off the neck. In the summertime, the wood absorbs moisture and tends to bow out, so that the strings are closer to the fingerboard. I always carry around an adjustment wrench to do any necessary tweaking. Sometimes, I even do it between takes, because to get the fingerboard to really buzz with that vibrant fretless sound requires constant adjustment. It can be a pain, but it's my musical voice and I wouldn't trade it for anything!

EGAN MUSIC

Mark Egan addresses playing a melody on fretless bass by discussing "Beyond Words," the title track of his 1992 third solo album: "'Beyond Words' is based on a theme I developed in my duo with [drummer] Danny Gottlieb. On the disc, I played the melody shown below on a Pedulla eight-string fretless. You can play it on any bass, but using a fretless opens up a whole world of expressive possibilities.

"When I play a melody, I usually position my right hand between the end of the fingerboard and the neck pickup because I like the warmth of the sound when I pluck there. My right-hand technique, for the most part, is standard two-finger alternation. With my left hand, I put my thumb in the middle of the back of the neck, which is the best position for strength and maximum reach. (That's especially important to me, because I have small hands.)

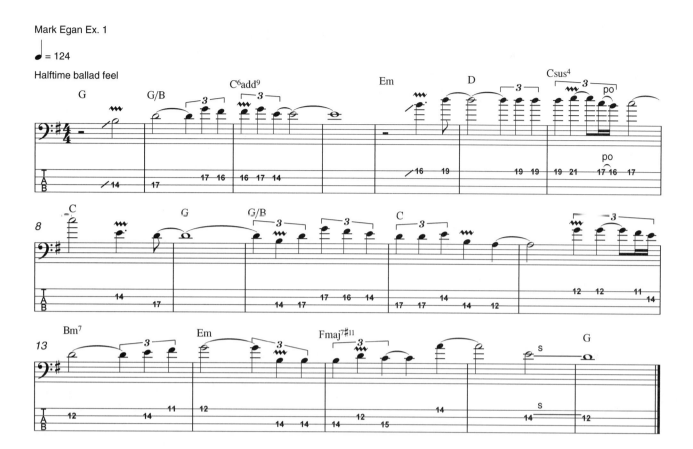

Mark Egan Ex. 1

♩ = 124

Halftime ballad feel

"I began 'Beyond Words' with a slide up to a B. When I start with a slide, I try to slide from a long way down—in this case, I slid from the F♯ on the D string (fourth fret) up to the B on the D string (ninth fret). I had to time the slide carefully so I arrived at the B exactly on the downbeat of three. I use many different types of slides, both ascending and descending. Sometimes I'll slide past a note and then reach back and articulate it; other times I'll slide up but play the target note on a different string. I also use many trills and hammers. Hammers are very important in melodic playing—if you pluck every note, your playing will sound stiff and monotonous; hammered notes flow more smoothly into each other. When I'm playing a lyrical melody like this one, I use a lot of slides and hammer-ons, with plucked notes reserved for accents.

"On fretless, vibrato is a crucial element; listen closely to 'Beyond Words,' and you'll notice that I use vibrato on many notes to make them 'sing.' I do this by placing my finger on the note and using it as a pivot point for rotating my hand; this is more like the side-to-side vibrato of a classical violinist than the up-and-down bending of a blues guitarist. Vibrato varies the pitch slightly, which gives the note more

color—and also helps you to adjust the intonation. Even on a fretless bass with inlaid markers, like my Pedulla, it's not enough just to put your finger on the line—or, more precisely, just behind the line. For one thing, your fingertip is wider and softer than a metal fret, so the point of contact is less defined. You also have to listen closely to the other instruments, especially if you're playing with a piano; because of the way pianos are tuned, you may be perfectly in tune with one register but out of tune with a higher or lower register. When that happens, you've got to adjust. I find that I'm constantly adjusting intonation in most playing situations—vigilance is a crucial part of the fretless experience!

"The highest note in this melody is the high E in bar 9. When I play that high on the neck, I bring my thumb around into a sort of modified thumb position; I find this to be a more comfortable position for upper-register playing.

"My fretless playing is like an extension of my singing voice. I begin with the sound of the melody in my head, and I play in phrases broken up with rests for 'breathing.' To play 'Beyond Words'—or any other fretless melody—I suggest you begin by singing through the music slowly. You don't have to be a great singer; this method will simply help you to understand the rhythm and the overall shape of the melody. Then, play the melody phrase by phrase. Begin with the first four measures; isolate the phrase, learn the rhythm, and find out where it lies best on your bass. Repeat that procedure for the entire melody. Once you've accomplished that, bring it up to tempo. Play along with the CD, or—even better—get someone to play the chords while you practice the melody. Pay close attention to your intonation—and enjoy yourself!"

ESSENTIAL GEAR

Assorted Pedulla Mark Egan Signature Buzz Basses (fretless four-, five-, and eight-strings); '64 Jazz Bass; D'Addario XL170 Nickel Roundwounds; Eden WT800B head and two D410XLT cabinets; Eventide H3000S Ultra-Harmonizer.

ESSENTIAL DISCOGRAPHY

Solo albums: *As We Speak*, Wavetone; *Freedomtown*, Wavetone; *Beyond Words*, Mesa/Bluemoon; *A Touch of Light*, GRP; *Mosaic*, Windham Hill. **With Elements:** *Spirit River*, RCA Novus; *Liberal Arts*, RCA Novus; *Illumination*, RCA Novus; *Blown Away*, Mesa/Bluemoon; *Forward Motion*, Antilles; *Elements*, Antilles. **With Sting:** *...Nothing Like the Sun*, A&M. **With Gil Evans:** *Live at Sweet Basil, Vols. 1 & 2*, Evidence. **With the Pat Metheny Group:** *American Garage*, ECM; *Pat Metheny Group*, ECM. **With Joan Osborne:** *Relish*, Mercury. **With Bill Evans:** *Living in the Crest of a Wave*, Blue Note. **With Sophie B. Hawkins:** *Tongues and Tails*, Columbia. **With Gil Goldstein:** *Wrapped in a Cloud*, Muse.

JIMMY HASLIP

by Alexis Sklarevski, Ed Friedland, and Chris Jisi

Jimmy Haslip (born December 31, 1951, in the Bronx, New York) is in his fourth decade as both an in-demand Los Angeles session bassist and cofounder of the Grammy-winning group Yellowjackets. It was with the Jackets that he forged a unique and expressive fretless style.

Looking back, why did you decide to become a bass player?

I grew up in a household where I heard a lot of music, and when I was a little kid the one style that really grabbed me was salsa. It had an infectious groove. I grew up listening to [bands led by] Machito, Tito Puente, Mongo Santamaria—all of the Latin artists. My older brother Gabriel turned me on to a lot of music; he was deeply into jazz and classical music. From my peers, I heard all the Motown and R&B stuff, and I was completely consumed with music. I started on drums when I was very small and played trumpet in elementary school. Then one night I was at a junior-high dance, and there was this band with an electric bass. That did it! It grabbed me and shook me, and I thought, "Wow, I like that!" I started out on a Japanese bass called a Zimgar; it cost fifty bucks. I had that for about a year, and I learned quite a few tunes on it. That really got me into the idea of playing bass.

Did you take lessons?

I got together with a guy named Ron Smith, who played tuba with Elvin Jones, and later I went to a small private music school for a bit. That didn't work out at all—the teacher didn't understand what I was doing. I'm naturally left-handed, so when I got a bass I just flipped it over and started figuring it out that way. The teacher kept telling me to play right-handed, but I didn't want to do that.

I made up my own rules as I went along. I've always played upside down, with my E string [at the bottom of the fingerboard] where the G string would be normally. At first, I just used my thumb—not slapping with it, just plucking. Then I started to pick with two fingers, which is the technique I still use most of the time.

When you started out, what bass players were you listening to?

James Jamerson was *the* influence at the time, although I didn't find out who he was until fifteen years later. And Paul McCartney, for two reasons: I loved the Beatles, and he played left-handed! Also Chris Squire from Yes, Peter Cetera from Chicago, Jack Bruce, Noel Redding, Jack Casady, Phil Lesh, and Berry Oakley. Oakley was really an inspiration, because he used a lot of modal ideas. I also listened to Ron Carter, Scott LaFaro, Jimmy Garrison, Reggie Workman, and other acoustic jazz players.

When and why did you start playing five- and six-string basses?

Let's see; I got to L.A. in 1975, so I started playing

five-string in 1985—but I didn't move on to the six-string until March of '91. Around 1983, I heard Jimmy Johnson at a club in L.A. Jimmy had been using a five-string for a long time, and I just loved the sound. There were all these great low notes coming out, and at first I thought he had some sort of pedal. Then I realized it was the bass itself.

Did you find the transition difficult?

Going from a four-string to a five-string was a bit of a chore, although I think a lot of it was psychological. Within a couple of months, I felt pretty comfortable playing it. Going from a five to a six was not nearly as hard.

When did you begin playing fretless?

I got my Tobias five-string fretless in 1987, and at first I used it very little due to the intonation problems. I practiced hard that whole year, and by 1988, when the Yellowjackets went in to do the *Politics* album, I used it on that. I also played it on a Gino Vannelli tune called "Wild Horses" [*Big Dreamers Never Sleep*].

The more I worked with it, the more I decided to dedicate myself to the fretless bass. After *Politics* came out we went on tour, and I brought only the fretless—it was a sink-or-swim situation! I spent five months on the road playing fretless, and by the end of that year I felt I had a handle on it.

What did you do to develop your fretless sound?

At first, I had to concentrate on intonation. I met Jaco in the '70s, when he had just joined Weather Report, and I took a few lessons from him. One of the things he taught me was to put the fingertip of your fretting hand right on the fret marker to get the true note. The center of your finger has to be right on the line. Once I got a feel for the intonation, I started working on my vibrato. Mstislav Rostropovich, the master cellist, was a big inspiration for that technique—he's truly incredible!

How big an influence was Jaco?

I was certainly inspired by him. I listened to him quite a bit, not to copy his playing, but just to learn more about playing fretless. As time went by, I realized how expressive the instrument could be.

Jaco was a master. I really liked him, not only as a musician and a composer, but also as a person. We ran into one another many times on the road, and I always felt he was my friend. He did so much for *all* musicians, not just bass players. He had a special place in my heart, and when he passed away I was very disturbed.

My book, *The Melodic Bass Library*, is dedicated to Jaco and James Jamerson. Those two guys, along with

Anthony Jackson, were huge influences on my playing. I don't think I sound like any of them, though; we all have our own personalities.

You were credited with playing fretless on Gino Vannelli's *Brother to Brother*, but you didn't start playing fretless until nine years after the record came out. How did you get that sound on a fretted bass?

I used a very quick hammer-on technique leading to the note I wanted to ring—it's like a fast series of grace notes preceding a specific pitch. With a little chorus, it becomes even smoother. By the time I did that record I'd already hung out with Jaco, and I wanted to emulate the sound of a fretless.

You're very good at phrasing. How did you develop that?

I listened to horn players and guitarists. A lot of it has to do with the way I hear music and how I incorporate that into the way I play. Going back to Jaco again, one thing he told me was that he studied players like Charlie Parker, Miles Davis, and John Coltrane because they had the best phrasing.

What goes on in your head when you're soloing?

I don't want to think of anything in the moment. I'd say it's a true connection between my heart and my soul. I have some ideas about how I'd like to approach the solo, but truthfully, I have no preconception of what will actually happen in the improvisation state. I practice at least four hours a day; that's a good time to analyze and concentrate on phrasing, melody, patterns, and tonality. I believe practicing will prepare you for open improvisation. Consciously, I'm listening to the accompaniment, the form of the solo section, the rhythms, and things that might inspire me to instantly interact with what's happening. But the bottom line is the solo has to be expressive; I want to express my emotions, whether it's sadness, joy, anger, fear, or love. That doesn't mean it has to be technically perfect.

You play left-handed with the bass strung upside down. How has that affected your style?

In some way it's given me a different perspective looking at musical patterns, and in some ways perhaps a small technical advantage. I've never felt normal playing this way, that's for sure! But then again, I don't spend a lot of time thinking about how I play. I like to submerge myself in the music and set myself free to express the music the way I hear it.

Does the stringing make it harder to play "normal" material?

Not at all. At one time I thought it would hinder my playing, but eventually I saw anything is possible—even upside down. It boils down to your confidence and how much you really want to play the music. I do have to practice a lot to learn some of the music I'm playing, just because it's hard no matter how you play the instrument. If you want to play challenging material, you have to spend time learning and assimilating it. If you're having difficulty with something, play it slowly and build yourself up to speed—it's the best way to learn difficult music.

How have you grown as a bassist and musician over the last twenty-five years?

Overall, the most important aspect is that I have a stronger vision as an artist. It comes down to needing good compositions to advance your musicianship, and I've been fortunate to be around people like Russell and Bob Mintzer. That has enabled me to grow measurably as a writer and also as a producer, because we're meticulous about our recorded sound.

Playing-wise, my knowledge of feels, harmony, and soloing has gone up several notches, as has my string count! I started on four-string, went to five in the mid '80s, had a six by 1990, and I even did a tour on seven-string. Plus, I played fretless almost exclusively from 1989 to 1998. During that period I studied upright players like Ron Carter, Cecil McBee, Dave Holland, and Charlie Haden, and that opened me up to other possibilities. Acoustic bassists play with a lot of girth, which gives them a fatter sound and greasier groove. That led me to play with a more acoustic approach: using fewer notes and being more spontaneous and flowing when improvising bass lines. The band's penchant for polyrhythmic figures and odd time signatures has also enhanced my playing. And I'm constantly motivated to learn more. It's like the old saying: the more you know, the more you realize how much you don't know!

What has been the one constant throughout the Yellowjackets' history?

Russell and I have a mirrored vision of the band and the music. We set a precedent for keeping the music collaborative and open, and for not being afraid to try new ideas, for better or for worse. It has been a wonderful laboratory for all who have been involved. The future for us is to stay the course in striving to create music that both challenges and touches listeners. In addition, with the amount of clinics and residencies we now do, we have serious careers as educators to uphold.

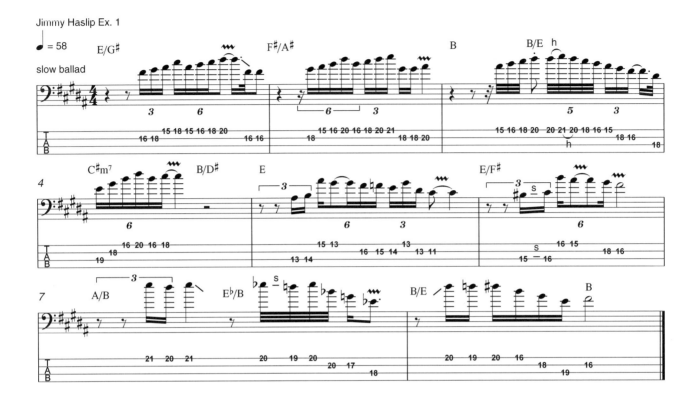

Jimmy Haslip Ex. 1

♩ = 58
slow ballad

HASLIP MUSIC

Jimmy Haslip turns to his composition "Galileo (for Jaco)," from the 1992 Yellowjackets album, *Politician*, for a lesson: "My fretless solo on 'Galileo' is a good example of how you can use modal scales to create melodies. Here's some background: The seven modal scales are all derived from the major scale, and each mode has its characteristic sound. The modes are formed by taking the notes in any major scale and building new scales, one beginning on each scale degree. The seven modal scales will provide you with endless combinations of notes to create different-sounding phrases and melodic patterns. At the same time, you will always be using the notes of a major scale. Technically speaking, you can solo over a major chord and by using, say, a Dorian or a Locrian scale, build a melodic phrase with a minor sound. This gives the major chord a more interesting color or mood.

"With this in mind, I suggest playing slowly through my solo on 'Galileo' and listening carefully to the way it sounds. The song is in the key of B, and my solo is based largely on the notes in the B-major scale: B, C♯, D♯, E, F♯, G♯, A♯, B. Make a tape of the chords and play along with it. How does each phrase sound against the chord? How does it make you feel? Once you've done that, analyze the phrases and try to determine which modal scales I used.

The example below is the final eight bars of the solo. You'll notice that the one place where I deviated from the diatonic sound is in bars 7–8 (the next-to-last line), where the chord progression creates a kind of false turnaround. I was looking at the A/B as a B7sus, the E♭/B as a Bmaj7♯5 (thus the G♮), and the B/E as an Emaj7. That added a little spice to the sound, and then I shifted back to B major. Once you've worked through what I played on this tune, take the same scales and create your own melodies. Have fun!"

ESSENTIAL GEAR

Tobias fretless five- and six-strings; Roscoe fretted six-string; D'Addario Prisms strings; SWR 550x or 750x head with Goliath III 4x10 cabinet.

ESSENTIAL DISCOGRAPHY

With the Yellowjackets (on Warner Bros. except where noted): *Mint Jam*, Yellowjackets; *Club Nocturne*; *Dreamland*; *Like a River*, GRP; *Greenhouse*, GRP; *Politics*, MCA; *Samurai Samba*; *Mirage à Trois*; *Yellowjackets*. **With Gino Vannelli:** *Big Dreamers Never Sleep*, Epic; *Black Cars*, CBS Associated; *Brother to Brother*, A&M. **With Robben Ford:** *The Inside Story*, Elektra. **With Anita Baker:** *Rapture*, Elektra. **With Steely Dan:** *Gold*, MCA. **With Bruce Hornsby:** *Hot House*, RCA.

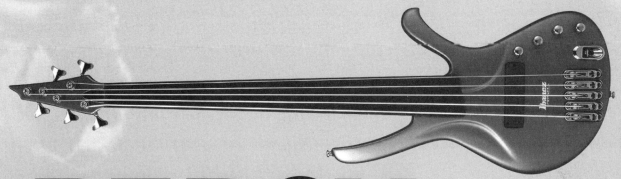

PERCY JONES

by Sean Gerety and Chris Jisi

Few players have made more of an impact on the vocabulary of the fretless bass than Percy Jones (born December 3, 1947, in Abbey Cwmhir, Powys County, Wales). Forged with Brand X in the '70s, his angular, aggressive style was one of the few viable alternatives to the pervasive influence of Jaco. He remains one of the instrument's most singular and important explorers.

Welsh Rare Bass

Jones, who grew up in rural central Wales, showed little interest in any kind of music early on, even after the piano lessons his mother gave him at age eight. By the early '60s, though, as Percy reached his mid teens, the rock bands that began to replace dance bands on local gigs caught his ear. He recalls, "I was fascinated by the electric bass, and I don't really know why. I suppose the low range attracted me, and visually I liked the four long, thick strings; plus, the concept of working with the drummer appealed to me. I thought, I'd like to have a go at that." He continues, "There was a guy in town who actually had an electric bass, which was pretty rare at that time. It was a cheesy Vox Clubman with plastic tuners, and he wanted ten quid for it. I got the money from my mom and proceeded to try to teach myself how to play, since there were no teachers around. I learned by playing along with rock and R&B records by the Yardbirds, Chuck Berry, the Hollies, the Who, Alexis Korner, John Mayall and the Bluesbreakers, and American blues artists."

Liverpool Scene

Moving to Liverpool in 1966 to attend the University of Liverpool as an electronic engineering student, Jones met many of the city's musicians. He eventually left school and joined a band called the Liverpool Scene, a sort of beatnik improv group with folk guitar, bass, drums, and sax, set up around poet/vocalist Adrian Henri. Percy remembers, "The sax player, Mike Evans, played me a Charles Mingus record—and it was a revelation! I loved Mingus's wild energy and the unpredictability of his music from one moment to the next. I got every Mingus record I could, and I tried to copy his playing, too. At the time I had a Gretsch hollowbody, and I filed down the frets under the *G* string so I could pull it off the fingerboard like he did."

The Liverpool Scene evolved into more of a rock band and became quite popular, leading to several albums, a series of live TV shows, an English tour with Led Zeppelin, and a U.S. tour that culminated in Percy meeting Mingus himself in New York. "I went to see him play," Jones smiles, "and afterward I approached him for a lesson. He was very nice, but he turned me down because I played electric bass." With the breakup of the Liverpool Scene, Jones moved to London in 1971 to test the musical waters. While working at construction and electronics jobs, he continued to draw on the influence of such upright players as Paul Chambers and Jimmy Garrison and the music of Miles Davis and John Coltrane. "Then came fusion," Percy notes, "with Weather Report, Mahavishnu, Tony Williams's Lifetime, and Return to Forever. When I heard them I thought, 'This is what I want to do.'"

Brands X

Brand X had a dual beginning and a dual ending. Its inception occurred in 1974 when Jones, who was living in South London, met keyboardist Robin Lumley, who invited Percy to move into a large house he shared with several other musicians. Lumley also brought Jones to a weekly rehearsal he ran, which included guitarist John Goodsall. Almost immediately, the group clicked. One of the members got the new band an audition for Island Records, and much to everyone's surprise, they were signed. Brand X, as they dubbed themselves, recorded a vocal album which Percy describes as "the Below-Average White Band." Before its release, Lumley, Goodsall, and Jones got label permission to record an instrumental fusion album instead. They changed personnel accordingly, adding drummer Phil Collins at the label's suggestion. Oddly, Island didn't like the new record and dropped the band. Fortunately, Collins brought the record to Genesis's label, Charisma, which released *Unorthodox Behaviour* in 1976.

Six weeks before recording the album, Percy bought a used sunburst fretless Precision with his $200 publishing advance. He recalls, "I instantly fell in love with it, even though I was struggling with my intonation. It answered my need for the expressive qualities of the upright with the volume and attack of the electric. I knew I had to play it on the album, so I worked 'round the clock to get it together. I used open strings and harmonics as reference points to help my intonation." What else contributed to the band's unique sound? "I think it was our wide collective influences and our European heritage," surmises Jones. "We were heavily inspired by the quality of playing and writing of the American fusion bands, but we didn't try to copy anything specific. The funny thing was that we were much more popular in the U.S.—the birthplace of fusion—than we were in Europe. Lumley used to say, 'It's like bringing coal to Newcastle.'"

Successive classic albums, including *Moroccan Roll*, *Livestock*, and *Masques* (for which Percy switched to Wal basses), found the band gravitating from group writing to individual writing. With nothing charted, members memorized their parts and relied on head cues to change sections or to begin and end improvisational flights. The strong sense of groove present throughout can be credited to

Collins and Jones, who always kept the foundation close at hand to fall back on when needed.

Critical success aside, mounting pressure from both the label and management to produce more accessible music had divided the band by 1979. Jones felt that compromising the music would not only fail to attract a new audience, it would also drive away the old one. Lumley and Collins thought it was a good idea, and Goodsall sat on the fence. As a result, Brand X's final two group recordings, *Product* and *Do They Hurt?*, were actually done with two separate bands recording in shifts. Lumley, Collins, and Goodsall enlisted John Giblin on fretless bass, while the more progressive material featured Jones, Goodsall, Herbie Hancock drummer Mike Clarke, and Masques keyboardist Peter Robinson. "Everything was quite cordial," Percy hastens to explain. "John Giblin and I even recorded a duet called 'Wal to Wal' on *Product*."

An Englishman in New York

Seeking a new, more supportive musical environment while also providing his wife with an opportunity to return to her native Manhattan, Jones moved to New York City in the fall of 1979. Brand X played its final tour in 1980, during which Percy received a call from guitarist John McLaughlin to join his road band. Jones laments, "I turned down John because we were supposed to go back out with Brand X; then management called to say our label had dropped us for financial reasons, effectively breaking up the band." Percy's Gotham career started via an invitation to jam with what would become the avant-garde group Paranoise, extended to him when he met one of the members in a supermarket. This introduction to the burgeoning "downtown" scene paved the way for Percy to form Stone Tiger, a trio with Mike Clarke and guitarist Bill Frisell. It also enabled Jones to land sideman gigs with such Knitting Factory regulars as multi-instrumentalist Elliot Sharp, saxophonist Tim Berne, and drummer Bobby Previte.

Another result was Jones's first solo album, *Propeller Music*, which he recorded in 1984—although he had to wait six years before the disc was released on Hot Wire. In 1985, Sharp hired Percy for a series of solo bass gigs, for which he accompanied himself with machines. This led to three years of live solo performances with MIDI gear, culminating in his second solo album, *Cape Catastrophe*. Looking to return to playing with other musicians, Jones was introduced to drummer Frank Katz by Mike Clarke, and he met vibist

Marc Wagnon soon after. In 1990, the trio added guitarist Van Manakas and named themselves Tunnels; a self-titled album was released on Ozone three years later. Ozone also re-teamed Percy with John Goodsall after a twelve-year separation for the first Brand X "reunion" album, 1992's *X-Communication*, with Frank Katz on drums. Last year, Goodsall's management enlisted Jones for *Manifest Destiny*, Percy bringing along his Tunnel-mates Katz and Wagnon.

Percy vs. Pastorius

Percy's fretless fusion peers Alphonso Johnson and Fernando Saunders made successful transitions to the pop world, while his fellow Welsh bassists Pino Palladino and Laurence Cottle have enjoyed thriving session careers. So has Percy passed on similar offers, or have they passed on him? "Both," he casually replies. "I know some people on the scene thought my playing was too busy. On the other hand, Phil Collins inquired if I was interested in joining Genesis; I also auditioned for Roxy Music, and Peter Gabriel called me for a tour, but I was unavailable. Though none of those situations worked out, I wouldn't have been opposed to doing gigs that are musically enjoyable *and* pay the rent. But I have no regrets about the path of my career. The only time I get bent out of shape is when I'm accused of being a clone."

Alluding to the unavoidable comparisons to Jaco Pastorius, whom he met while both were teaching at the Drummers Collective in the early '80s, Jones explains, "I'm a huge fan of Jaco's, and though I had established a style of my own by the time I first heard him, he definitely had an influence on me. Sonically, I was taken with his high-end tone and articulation, and musically he inspired me to try to be more melodic. But accusations that I was a poor Jaco copy were a bit upsetting and unfair. I can see the similarities—we both play fretless and use harmonics—but our sound and styles are different. He comes from more of a bebop/R&B area. What's most disappointing is that people don't let the music speak for itself."

Does Percy, in turn, hear himself in other bassists? "Yes, in clubs, on CDs, and on the radio—and it's extremely flattering. Mick Karn, for example, has been very kind in acknowledging my influence on him. Those sorts of things keep me going and more than make up for the clone comments."

Horizontal Insight

While playing his fretted Gretsch bass in the early '70s, Jones first discovered and used harmonics in conjunction

Percy Jones Ex. 1

♩ = 125

Fast funk

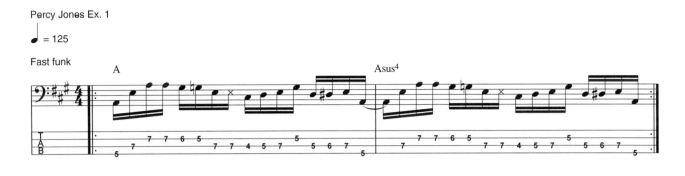

Percy Jones Ex. 2

♩ = 92

Swung funk

with fundamental tones to give his chords a wider range. With his switch to a fretless P-Bass in 1974 came the addition of vocal-like vibrato, whooping slides, sliding harmonics, artificial harmonics, and chordal harmonics. Since moving to extended-range basses and tuning his *B* string up a half-step to C "to shake up the ascending fourths pattern," Percy has developed some fascinating new techniques. These include pulling his C or G string off the side of the fingerboard, à la Charles Mingus, to produce a "near-offensive rattle"; scraping the lower string of a sliding chord with his thumbnail to produce a "pitched scratch"; striking the body or the back of the neck with his knuckles to sound overtones; playing an octave and fingering a false harmonic on the lower note, creating a "disturbing unison sound" with the top note; gently placing a fingertip under a plucked open string, which, at various points, "will trigger anything from a harmonic to a raucous buzz"; mixing muted and non-muted notes on rapid arpeggios; and using his left-hand thumb to fret notes "upright-style" on the upper por-

tion of the fingerboard in order to free his fingers to reach wide intervals. He laughs, "I'll try anything to make the bass sound like it usually doesn't."

As for his ability to move effortlessly from groove to fill to melody line, Percy credits his minimalist compositional style, which often exposes his bass as the lone voice. "My writing tends to be linear and horizontal—sort of slender in shape with contrapuntal themes as opposed to dense, vertical harmonies. If I use chords, they rarely have more than three notes." He continues, "Usually, I'll get an idea of a tempo and a feel, and then I'll sit at a keyboard and start messing around until I hear something interesting to elaborate on. It can be a melody, a progression, or even something sonic—a certain sound. From there, I'll go back and forth between my bass, the drum track, and other sequenced parts, and allow the tune to grow organically."

R.I.P., Rock & Roll?

Percy is anxious to dig into Tunnels again for some live

shows here and abroad. Addressing a more general goal, he states, "Ultimately, I'd like to come up with a whole new concept of how a rhythm section functions. We're still locked into the bass matching the kick and playing off of the hi-hat. On 'Stellerator,' I experimented with putting the bass on the downbeats and the kick on the upbeats. That's a very rudimentary example, but there's a need to explore different ways of putting the bass and drums together."

Contemplating the broader possibilities, Jones continues, "I think rock & roll is finally dying after more than thirty years of being the most popular music, and I'm glad. We're overdue for a change. A lot of young listeners are rebelling against rock; they're into techno or industrial—something that's sonically different, even if it's on a superficial level artistically. With synthesized music of this sort, traditional melodic, harmonic, and rhythmic functions are altered or abandoned. As these influences are adapted by creative musicians who play real instruments in real time, we'll gradually begin to turn the corner. I just hope I can be a part of it all."

JONES MUSIC

Percy Jones's commitment to creativity enables his unique bass voice to be heard throughout *Manifest Destiny*—whether he's interpreting a sequenced bass part, as on "True to the Clik"; cowriting with his fellow band members, as on the title track; or recording one of his own compositions, as on "The Worst Man." "Manifest Destiny," written by Brand X during rehearsals for the recording sessions, fades out on a repeating two-bar section contributed by Jones. (See Ex. 1.) This segment begins at the 3:34 mark of the track, following a rubato synth interlude. Explains Percy, "I had been working on a steady sixteenth-note groove that was inspired by Rocco Prestia from Tower of Power, and I sort of tagged it onto the end of the tune. On the record, the accent is on the last sixteenth of beat four—but live, Frank and I have been throwing in additional accents in different places."

Ex. 2 is the four-bar phrase from Jones's "The Worst Man"; it shows the original line he wrote for the song's A section. The phrase first appears at the track's 0:21 mark and repeats eight times, with Jones altering the line—especially in the fourth measure—each time he plays it. Note the D Locrian tonality—an E♭ major scale starting on D, the scale's seventh degree. (The C♯s in bar 1 are lower approach-note passing tones, while the open E-string pickups to bars 1, 2, and 3 are ghosted and have no actual pitch.) Remember, Percy tunes his B string up a half-step to C. (This can be heard in bars 2, 3, and 4.) He reveals, "The song is named for a rip-off record executive I had the misfortune of being involved with. The C section is based on a piece called 'Noddy Goes to Sweden,' which I wrote in 1980 for the *Do They Hurt?* album."

ESSENTIAL GEAR

Ibanez custom wood Ergodyne five-string fretless (piezo pickups only); Ibanez AFR fretless five-string; Wal fretless; fretless early-'70s P-Bass; DR Lo-Riders; Euphonic Audio iamp 800C combo.

ESSENTIAL DISCOGRAPHY

Solo albums: (both on Hot Wire) *Cape Catastrophe*; *Propeller Music*. **With Brand X:** *Manifest Destiny*, Cleopatra; *Xcommunication*, *Ozone*. On Charisma: *Is There Anything About?*; *Do They Hurt?*; *Product*; *Masques*; *Livestock*; *Moroccan Roll*; *Unorthodox Behavior*. **With Tunnels** (all on Buckyball): *Natural Selection*; *Progressivity*; *Tunnels*; *Painted Rock*. **With Brian Eno:** *Music for Films*, Antilles; *Before and After Science*, Polydor; *Another Green World*, Island. **With Suzanne Vega:** *Days of Open Hand*, A&M.

ALAIN CARON

by Bill Milkowski and Peter Murray

A true Canadian music and bass god, Alain Caron (born 1955, in Quebec, Canada) is an impeccable fretless bassist with a gift for jazz, funk, and any other genres and grooves he chooses to grace. From his fusion trio UZEB to his solo recordings and sideman work, he somehow remains and underrated bass force.

How did you come to play bass?

I started to play in clubs when I was very young, around eleven years old. I began by playing guitar and drums and only switched over to bass when a bandleader asked me to give it a try. He was an ex-bass player who had an old Fender Jazz Bass. He wanted me to do some piano/bass duets with him during the set, so I tried it. I fell in love with the instrument right away because it was the perfect blend of the two things I was already familiar with: it was a drum and a guitar at the same time.

Who were your influences?

Well, I discovered jazz soon after, and Ray Brown made a big impression. At first, I couldn't understand what he was doing. When he soloed, he would play notes that were far away from the root. I was determined to find out what he was doing, so I bought every instructional book I could find and began studying privately with piano players and sax players to get an understanding of jazz theory. I got to the point where I was playing upright at a dozen jazz clubs with all the bebop musicians in town.

When I heard Jaco's first album, I thought, "What the hell is that?" But right after [Weather Report's] *Heavy Weather* [Columbia, 1977] came out, I kind of stopped listening to Jaco. I went back to my roots and listened to upright bassists like Ray and Scott LaFaro again. And I started to work on my sound a great deal, trying to get away from that Jaco sound, because everybody who played fretless at that time was accused of trying to sound like Jaco. I wanted to keep on playing fretless, but I had another sound in my head—one that was a lot smoother, with not as strong an attack as Jaco's. I think finally I am developing my own voice on the instrument. I don't have Jaco's sound or Jaco's approach anymore. Jaco's influence, yes, that will always be there—but I feel I am finding my own thing now.

How did UZEB form?

When I was twenty-one, I met [guitarist] Michel Cusson, and we moved to Montréal, where we hooked up with [drummer] Paul Brocho to form a band. Our name was a complete joke; the first time we played was on St. Euzebe Day, so they called it the St. Euzebe Jazz Party. It's ridiculous! As we gained recognition and a record deal, we knew we needed a proper name. After searching and searching, we decided to keep just the four middle letters: UZEB. I thought it was a cool, weird name—and everybody who already knew us was able to relate.

How important was being a member of a band in developing your sound and style, as opposed to being a session player?

It's very tough to be in a band, because the better a musician gets, the more the phone rings. So, first of all, it's hard to get a

schedule together; when you're trying to book a band, the members have to be available. UZEB's main virtue was that everybody was focused on the band, so it allowed us to book gigs and try things at different levels: music, performance, developing a unique sound, producing records, managing tours—all the parameters that are important in a career. It's good to be able to go into a studio where they say, "Here's the chart, the style is this, I want you to go in that direction"—but it's not in those situations that you develop your sound. The main thing I got out of UZEB was the ability to develop my sound and spread the word.

Why did you decide to put "Donna Lee" on your CD *Rhythm 'n' Jazz*, instead of covering a different Charlie Parker tune or a Jaco composition?

I realize you've got to be pretentious to do that! [*Laughs.*] I thought about it a long time. I was already practicing all the Parker heads when Jaco came on the scene—but the way he did it was so strong, so musical, and so good that I'll always have respect for him. I practiced "Donna Lee" on fretless, to prove to myself I was able to do it; then I started to do it on the upright, in the same register; and then I started to practice it an octave higher. Finally, I played it with my slap technique: I thought, "I'll practice it just for me"—but at some point I decided it was good. In the liner notes, though, I wrote that the tune was for Jaco, because it doesn't belong to me. I can play "Donna Lee" on fretless and make it sing a lot more, but that's been done; I figured my version had to be unique. I think I've done that, whether you like it or not. I must confess I like it, and I'm still working on it!

You have fantastic intonation on fretless. Are there specific exercises you worked on to develop that?

I'm still working on it. The main thing is to want it, to make it your top priority—even more than the actual notes you're playing. When you play, you need a lot of experience with the instrument to be able to disconnect yourself and be your own listener. I practice slowly, and the thing that has helped me the most is practicing lots of solo pieces, like Bach's. You should first get in tune with yourself—from one note to another—and then get in tune with the other players. I've found that if I start to listen to the notes I play instead of the pitches, I get out of tune; it's all a matter of focus. I've also found it's harder to play in tune through headphones.

When I first got a computer a long time ago, I started to practice scales and arpeggios just for intonation, with no vibrato at all: playing all the notes right on the buck. I taped myself and listened back to it. Left-hand technique is very important for intonation; as you improve your technique, your intonation will get better.

Your thumbstyle playing has become more and more even between the slaps and pops. When did you start

Alain Caron Ex. 1

developing that concept, and how did you make it happen?

I've always had that concept. When I started listening to Stanley Clarke, the thing I noticed was that most slappers didn't play melodies—just octaves and rhythmic things on basic chord tones. I started to work on octaves, but right away I also started to slap in upstrokes as well as downstrokes and to pull with both my index and middle fingers. There's an example of that on a tune called "Brass Licks," on UZEB's first studio record [*Fast Emotion*]; not many players were using that technique at the time, which was in 1981. For the past five years I've spent a lot of time on my slapping, and I'm still splitting my time half-and-half between fretless and slap.

What would you say to a young player who's trying to improve?

You should always have fun, first of all. For many years I was never happy, because I was always trying to reach next month's level, which was impossible. If your friends tell you you're good, it's not good enough. Go challenge yourself. When you think you're good, go practice—listen to Jaco's "Donna Lee" or Scott LaFaro. But you have to be careful not to go too far on the other side and think you're shit; that's dangerous, too. Play at your own level. If you practice something during the day, don't try to play it that night, because you'll be disappointed. In general, I'd say you've got to be proud of yourself, so you can do what you do with conviction. You have to be convinced of what you can do.

CARON MUSIC

Alain Caron's composition "Slinky," from UZEB's 1982 disc, *Fast Emotion*, captures his Jaco-like ability to groove hard and expressively on the fretless. He recalls, "I remember working on octaves at that point; specifically using my first and third fingers followed by my second and fourth fingers to pluck two octaves in a row. Plus, I was doing a lot of disco sessions at the time, so octaves were on my brain!" Examples 1, shows the one-bar repeated ostinatos of the song's A, B, and C sections. Alain offers, "Slowly practice getting the octave sixteenths even and grooving, so that your right hand can adjust to and control the large intervals. Also be aware that the last two sixteenths of beat two, in Examples 1 and 2, need to be locked with the drummer."

ESSENTIAL GEAR

Fretless and fretted F Bass Alain Caron signature six-strings; LaBella strings; two Roland D-Bass 210 2x10 combo amps with two Roland D-Bass 115X 1x15 extension speaker cabinets.

ESSENTIAL DISCOGRAPHY

Solo albums: *Live at the Cabaret de Montréal*, Norac/Ghost Note; *Rhythm 'n' Jazz*, Avant-Garde/Lipstick; *Le Band*, Avant-Garde. **With UZEB** (all on Disques Avant-Garde): *Live in Bracknell*; *World Tour 90*; *UZEB Club*; *Live in Europe*; *Noisy Nights*; *Between the Lines*; *Fast Emotion*. **With Caron-Ecay-Lockwood:** *Caron*, *Ecay*, *Lockwood*, Avant-Garde. **With Leni Stern** (both on Lipstick): *Like One*; *Ten Songs*.

BUNNY BRUNEL

by Ed Friedland

*Bernard "Bunny" Brunel (born March 2, 1950, in Nice, France)
unleashed his distinctive fretless wail in the midst of the fusion-
borne bass revolution—no easy task. He has remained one of the
instrument's important figures.*

How did you arrive at bass?

I started on piano at age nine. About four years later [1963], I was playing guitar in the school band when the director sent me on an errand to rent an acoustic bass for the new bass player. When I got back he told me the bass player wasn't going to join the band and asked why didn't I play it? I loved it, and after a couple of weeks I was the best in town. I figured I might as well stick with it—it was easier than guitar! I began teaching myself on a borrowed electric, and by the early '60s I was doing R&B, rock, and jazz gigs in southern France. I moved to Paris in the early '70s, where I started doing gigs and studio work with the top jazz musicians around.

When did you get started playing fretless?

When the Music Man StingRay came out, I bought one to keep as a fretted bass and took the frets off my '65 Precision. I filled the slots with Bondo—I really butchered the thing. I had somebody put a finish on the fingerboard, and that was it.

Who were your early influences?

The first bass player I noticed was Willie Dixon. I used to listen to those old-style "mystery" bass solos that were more like drum solos, because they weren't playing any changes. I liked piano players such as Herbie Hancock and Chick Corea—I wanted to solo that way, and to solo more like saxophone players. I loved John Coltrane, so I started trying to play phrases. One day a friend played me a record of Eddie Gomez. I thought, "I want to play like that!" From there I went back and heard Scott LaFaro and Gary Peacock. Back then nobody was soloing on the electric bass like that. I also loved all the James Brown bass players; the groove and the lines were great. Then I got into Blood, Sweat and Tears—Jim Fielder was very inventive. Of course, there were also Carol Kaye—though I didn't know it was a girl playing—and James Jamerson on the Motown hits. Then I heard Stanley Clarke on the acoustic bass. I wanted to make it sound like that and yet solo like Gomez. I was working on my own thing when a friend played me the first Jaco record and said, "Listen to this guy—he sounds like you." My reaction was, "Shit, somebody did it before me!"

I finally met Jaco at the Roxy in L.A. I was playing with Tony Williams, and Jaco came down with his bass to say hi to Tony—he was in Tony's band just before me. He was going to sit in but he didn't. I asked why and he said, "You played—I didn't need to." It was really nice of him to give me such a compliment. I love Jaco; he brought a lot of melody into bass playing. He was a great musician, composer, everything. He was a genius.

What was it like working with Chick Corea when that kind of music was new?

It was a dream come true. I knew all of Chick's albums by heart—it was the music I knew best. Because of my musical upbringing, I consider myself a fusion player—I had to play many different styles, and I incorporate them all when I play. That's why all my albums have a little of everything in them. I don't know if it's good or bad, but everybody should be able to find something they like.

What's your approach to creating a bass line in an intense, hard-hitting atmosphere?

Well, I always try to create a groove behind the soloist, but I also keep a dialogue going on with the drummer and the soloist, giving different rhythms and little melodic lines. It helps soloists be creative and avoid monotony or static playing.

What advice can you offer with regard to intonation on the fretless?

To play in tune on the fretless, it's very important to have the fingers of your left hand parallel to the frets on the fingerboard. Also, the tip of the finger should not be centered on the mark of the fret. If you are right on it you will be too sharp. You should have only three-quarters of the tip of the finger on the place of the fret. For that, I definitely recommend fret markers. A bass with no markers may look good but usually the pitch gets bad.

How did you decide to go beyond being a sideman and take control of your career?

Well, I never found anyone who was willing to do it for me, so I'm doing it myself. It's a tough job. When you're a bassist and leader, people don't want to call you for bass sessions. They don't want a soloist; they want someone to lay down a groove—even though you *can* do that. Brian Bromberg and Stanley will tell you the same thing. And if you look at Jaco's life, except for the people who used him to sell their albums, nobody called him for session work. Fortunately some people call me because they know I can play the bass. For the *Highlander* series I even got to improvise some bass cues.

After playing for thirty-seven years, how do you stay musically fresh?

The secret is to practice a lot and not do what most people do. I went through my whole life, especially the '60s, with no drugs, no drinks, and not even too much coffee. People tend to associate music—especially jazz—with booze and drugs, but they don't help you play at all. Moderation is the key.

Bunny Brunel Ex. 1

♩ = 130

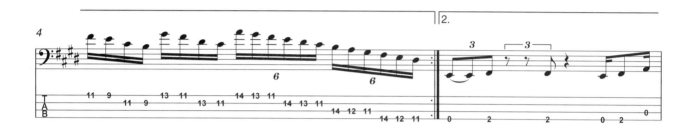

BRUNEL MUSIC

Excerpted from the title track of *CAB*, the debut disc by Bunny Brunel's supergroup with guitarist Tony MacAlpine, keyboardists Patrice Rushen and Brian Auger, and drummer Dennis Chambers, this thorny two-bar groove's over-the-top answer phrases make it even nastier. Ex. 1 shows answer phrases 5 and 6. Bunny wouldn't make any suggestions about where on the neck to play these licks. ("Figuring it out is the fun part.") Whether you follow our suggestions or work out your own fingerings, try to play these insane phrases as cleanly and quickly as Bunny does. The first lies pretty well on the neck; the fast triplets are a 4–3–1 finger pattern across all four strings. The second is mostly an F♯ minor pentatonic lick that breaks the pattern at the top and becomes E major pentatonic before returning to earth as a C augmented arpeggio. Beware the enharmonic B♯!

ESSENTIAL GEAR

Carvin Signature BB-70 fretless and fretted four-strings; BB-75 fretless and fretted five-strings; piccolo BB-75 piccolo; LaBella Hard Rockin' Steels and Slappers; two Carvin Cyclops combo amps.

ESSENTIAL DISCOGRAPHY

Solo albums: *Cafe Au Lait*, Brunel; *L.A. Zoo*, Tone Center; *Momentum*, Musidisc; *For You to Play*, Media 7; *Dedication*, Musidisc; *Ivanhoe*, Inner City; *Touch*, Warner Bros. **With CAB:** *CAB 4*, Favored Nations; *CAB 2*, Tone Center; *CAB*, Tone Center. **With Brunel/Didier Lockwood:** *Zigzag*, WEA. **With Kazumi Watanabe:** *Kilowatt*, Gramavision. **With Chick Corea:** *Secret Agent*, Polydor; *Tap Step*, GRP. **With Gayle Moran:** *I Love You Now*, Warner Bros.

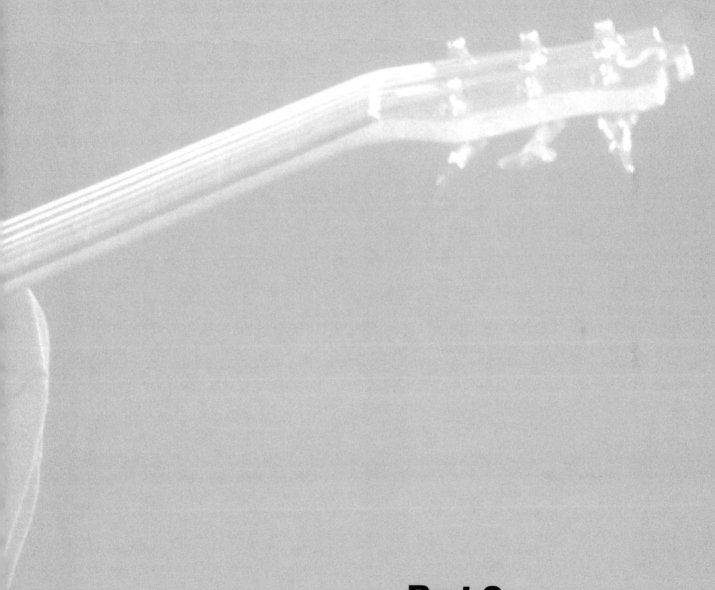

Part 3
Liquid Lessons

● ● ● ● ● ● ● ● ●

STEVE BAILEY

Over the past decade, Steve Bailey (born February 10, 1960, in Myrtle Beach, South Carolina) has become the grand master of the fretless six-string, noted cohort of Victor Wooten, and champion of all things bass. Early on in Bass Player, Steve really dug into his favorite instrument for his regular, always-entertaining column, Fretless Bass.

A Tale of Two Basses

Picture this: Jack has practiced for years, taken every gig he could get, lived on macaroni and cheese, and even gotten the dreaded day job so he could be the proud owner of two custom-made basses. Both have active electronics, neck-through-body construction, and all the other happenin' features Jack has fantasized about for years. But only one instrument sees the smoky clubs and dark studios, while the other sits lonely and forgotten in its gig bag. How come? It's a fretless.

Isn't it amazing that a few ounces of metal can make the difference between a happy, hardworking bass and a lonely, rejected, rusty-stringed closet dweller?

"Fretless bass" is a contradiction in terms. My dictionary says that *fret* means "to worry or vex," so *fretless* should mean "without worry," right? Then why is it that most of the bassists I know (including some household names) seem to worry quite a bit about being asked to play or—heaven forbid!—record on this instrument? The short answer to this long question: *intonation*.

A pivotal moment in my fretless career occurred when I was sixteen. After a brutal gig and a hurried load-out, my wonderful Spector fretted bass was the unfortunate victim of an altercation with the left rear wheel of my car. My only other bass was a fretless. I took it to the gig the following night and learned a great lesson. Not a single word was needed after I glanced at the keyboard player during a rousing version of "Under the Boardwalk." His expression said it all. Imagine, if you will, the look on a person's face after being lowered into a septic tank up to his neck. My intonation—or lack thereof—evoked that response, and his expression still turns up in my nightmares.

Many aspiring fretless players approach the study of the instrument much as most Americans approach the process of "getting in shape": eight hours at the gym the first day, no weight lost or muscle gained, an aching body . . . they quit. Intonation, like physical fitness, must be developed in a consistent, systematic way.

All of the beautiful nuances, warm tone, expressive phrasing, and melodic interpretation we associate with the fretless mean absolutely nothing if the notes are not in tune. Developing accurate pitch is a study that incorporates several different ingredients. Your ears, fingers, eyes, mind, and heart are all involved.

Ears: Ear training is essential. Developing good relative pitch narrows your margin of error.

Fingers: Good left-hand fingering habits are extremely important. A logical system emphasizing economy of motion and smooth, accurate shifting will make your intonation consistent everywhere on the fingerboard.

Eyes: Vision is probably your most valuable sense—except when you're playing fretless. Although your eyes are an indispensable aid to shifting accuracy and rough tuning, they become a problem when you use them as a crutch and rely on "seeing" your intonation. You can get so obsessed with watching your left hand that you can't read a chart or move around onstage, and pretty soon you don't even hear the other instruments—so how can you play in tune with them?

Mind: If your ears are the input and your hands are the output, then your mind is the processing center. The faster your mind "computes" whether you're flat or sharp, the quicker you can adjust your fingers.

Heart: Also known as "soul" or "taste." This is where your musicality comes from. When to slide up or down to a note, when to phrase a line as a melody or to play it with perfect meter, whether your vibrato sounds like a car alarm or a police siren (hopefully neither)—these are just a few of the things that come from within. These are also the things that are very difficult, if not impossible, to teach.

Intonation

How about a riddle? You've been lost in the desert for two days with no food or water, and you're dehydrated and delirious. Suddenly, three visions appear from behind a sand dune. One is a huge pink bunny rabbit. Another is an incredibly accurate, in-tune fretless bassist. The third is an out-of-tune, midrange-heavy, string-buzzing fretless bassist. Each gives you different directions to the nearest oasis. Which one do you believe? (Answer below.)

As a first step toward mastering the fretless bass, I'll present some exercises that will help you to get your intonation together. Warning: These exercises may seem boring, but they're actually deceptively difficult and require a good deal of left-hand conditioning.

In terms of hearing intonation, octaves are probably the easiest intervals to work with. Ex. 1 will help you to develop good pitch as well as left-hand consistency. I'm a devout supporter of the one-finger-per-fret (or fret-equivalent) rule as well as the extended fingering system (in which your left-hand fingers cover as many as five frets in one position), and you shouldn't have any problem with these systems above the fifth fret or so. Average-size or larger hands should have no problem using the first and third fingers in the lower positions after a bit of practice. If it seems difficult at first, stick with it—you'll be glad you did.

Let the notes sustain over each other, and listen for "beats" or "waves" in the sound, which indicate the notes are out of tune with one another. If they are, slightly roll one of your fingers to correct the pitch; you should strive to make these adjustments quicker and quicker. Also check your intonation against the open strings. For instance, when you land on a D, always check the pitch against that of open D.

Practice transposing Ex. 1 to different positions, and notice how your hand position "shrinks" as you move up the neck. Concentrate on memorizing how your hand feels in each position. And don't just play patterns—always be aware of what note you're playing. (Fingerboard knowledge never hurts.)

Ex. 2 is an exercise for fourths and fifths that will challenge your left hand (note the fingerings). Listen closely! As with the octaves, listen for "beats," which indicate that the notes are out of tune with each other. Let the tones ring as long as possible, and make your shifts smooth and seemingly effortless—silent if possible. Don't rush through these exercises until you can look straight ahead (not at your left hand) and play them in tune.

Let's now move on to thirds and tenths. The third is an effective device for solos, and it's great for adding spice and variety to bass lines. Thirds are generally most effective in the upper-mid to high registers. The tenth, as you probably know, is just a third with either the root dropped an octave or the top note raised an octave, depending on your perspective.

Ex. 3 consists of major and minor thirds. Play them over and over again, and really listen. Play them in tune, and play them out of tune. (Intonation is critical in thirds and tenths, since they define the major or minor tonality of the chord.) While holding the root, slide the third from major to minor, listening for that intonation "window." Notice the tension and release; the style of music as well as the other musicians will dictate exactly how in tune you need (or want) to be. Playing with synths and keyboards requires dead-on pitch, but guitars and horns are a little more flexible—especially when you're playing the blues. Fingering is critical here, as it's important to develop good spacing between all your fingers. Try to stay on your fingertips as well.

Your fingerings for tenths are optional, as they depend on where you're coming from and going to, musically. In general, I've found that playing the root with your second finger and the top note with the third or fourth finger works well, depending on whether the tenth is major or minor. I often finger major tenths 2–3, because that's how the notes lie under a major scale.

I frequently get asked which is better, a lined or unlined fingerboard. They're both fine, and I have no problem with lines as long as you don't rely on them completely. Ideally, the lines (and the dots on the sides of the neck) should be used only as reference points when shifting. Remember that the string bass, cello, and violin have no dots or lines. The students who play them need to rely heavily on their ears, since their eyes are reserved for reading the music and following the conductor.

Years ago, I thought I was a fairly accurate fretless bassist until one night when I was jamming with some friends and someone decided to turn off the lights so we could "get way into it." I went from confidence to chaos, and I realized I wasn't using my ears enough. The lesson is simple: Develop your ears! Try playing these exercises in the dark, and you'll be amazed at how quickly your ears and hands become great friends.

Here's the answer to the riddle: Trust the out-of-tune fretless bassist, because the other two are probably figments of your imagination.

Smoother Position Shifts

As you probably know by now, one large stumbling block in the quest for perfect intonation is position shifting. This problem is particularly bad while we're reading, because when we shift positions we not only lose the pitch but we often lose our place in the music as we look at our left hand. The following exercise (Ex. 4), which is an adaptation of what I call my "Hazard Exercises," will help you improve the accuracy of your position shifts and finger spacing, and give you stronger, more independent fingers. The hard part is what to do with your fingers after they're "finished." An asterisk over a note indicates that you should leave that finger where it is until you shift. Your index finger stays down (on the B) while your middle and ring fingers work their way back down; then your middle finger stays on the A while your ring finger and pinkie work their way back up. (Note that your index finger should still be holding down that B.) It gets worse before it gets better! As your pinkie plays the D, begin your smooth shift to the next position with your middle finger on the E♭, and work your way down. This time your index finger rests on B, your middle finger rests on D#, and your ring finger and pinkie struggle back down. Once your left hand gets

Steve Bailey Ex. 1

Steve Bailey Ex. 2

Steve Bailey Ex. 3

used to this, move down to the 1st position and work your way up the fingerboard. Be sure to check your pitch with open strings at the appropriate places.

One more note: Arch your fingers. This enables the force, or strength, generated by your forearm muscles to pass efficiently to your fingertips. Basketball, football, and baseball players—as well as pianists, typists, and massage therapists—all take advantage of this concept.

ESSENTIAL DISCOGRAPHY

Solo albums: *So Low ...Solo*, BATB; *Evolution*, JVC; *Dichotomy*, JVC. **With Victor Wooten:** *Palmystery*, Heads Up; *Soul Circus*, Vanguard; *Yin-Yang*, Compass. **With Bass Extremes:** *Just Add Water*, Tone Center; *Cookbook*, Tone Center. **With Jethro Tull:** *Roots to Branches*, Chrysalis. **With David Benoit:** *Inner Motion*, GRP. **With the Rippingtons:** *Curves Ahead*, GRP. **With Paquito D'Rivera:** *Live at the Keystone Corner*, Columbia.

MICHAEL MANRING

Michael Manring (born June 27, 1960, in Washington, D.C.) has long established himself as one of the bass guitar's leading experimentalists. From the beginning of his career, the fretless has been one of his favored test tubes. In addition to numerous cover and feature stories, Manring tackled some fretless topics in his regular late '90s Bass Player *column,* Alternatives.

Sliding Harmonics

I've been asked on several recording sessions to play chords or melodies using harmonics that just aren't available in the natural harmonics of my strings. One way to deal with the problem is to use a sliding-harmonic technique; it's most often associated with Bunny Brunel and Percy Jones, two masters of bass harmonics. Here's how it works: Recall that when a natural harmonic is activated, the string is set into a fractional vibration pattern; when the third harmonic is played, for example, the string vibrates in three equal subdivisions, with two "nodes" at the seventh and nineteenth frets. At these nodes, there is no string vibration, and the single string acts like three separate strings of equal length around these points. Now, if you play a third harmonic and then press the string to the fingerboard very gently at the seventh fret, where the string isn't moving, it's possible to allow the harmonic to continue sounding while you have the string closed. You can do the same thing by pressing down at the nineteenth fret, or even by pressing down at both the seventh and nineteenth frets simultaneously. This technique works best on a fretless instrument, but if you don't have one, don't despair—it does work on fretted basses, although it usually doesn't sound as pronounced. It takes a bit of practice to be able to press the string to the fingerboard without disrupting the harmonic vibration, but if you're interested in harmonics, this is a technique worth learning.

Once you have the string pressed to the fingerboard and the harmonic is still vibrating, you can change the pitch by sliding your fretting finger along the string, just as you would with a closed tone. Give it a try—it can open up a whole world of harmonic effects. This technique makes it possible to play harmonic vibrato and portamento, and, perhaps most important, it allows you to play harmonics that aren't in our original set.

Take a look at Ex. 1. Normally, you couldn't play this D major scale using natural harmonics, because there is no F# harmonic in the appropriate octave. However, you can play the E and then use the sliding-harmonic technique to move it up a whole-step to F#. To play the descending scale, slide the G down a half-step to F# and then continue on. The pitches of the slides correspond to the closed tones on the fingerboard, so if you slide the distance of a whole-step on the fingerboard, the harmonic pitch moves a whole-step. The trick is to remember that fourth, fifth, sixth, and seventh harmonics don't always produce the same notes as the closed tones in those positions, so in many cases you'll need

to do some quick transposing. For instance, if you slide the fourth harmonic at the fifth fret of the A string up a whole step, you'll hear B although your finger is on E.

It's important to note that I've presented the scale in Ex. 1 only to show how to play a pattern using sliding harmonics. In the musical real world, you'll probably want to use the technique for less rote musical phrases. Not all approaches will be stepwise, so practice sliding intervals larger than a whole-step. Also, the technique isn't necessarily just for playing harmonic pitches that aren't available as natural harmonics; you may want to slide to a note as a matter of phrasing preference or to simplify a fingering problem.

One more point: Don't feel you have to limit your slides to half- and whole steps. Ex. 2 shows an ascending, two-octave Amaj7 arpeggio using sliding harmonics. Here also, we're filling in the gaps in the available set of natural harmonics with slides. Again, the only choice for the first A is at the twelfth fret of the A string, so we'll slide up a major third from there to produce the following C#. There are a few options for the next four notes. I've included one way; you can figure out what works best for you. When we get to the E at the top of the treble-clef staff, there's only one option from the harmonics we've discussed so far: the sixth harmonic of the A string. If you play this note near the third fret and slide up a major third, your finger will end up on the E at the seventh fret, although you should hear a G#. (It's pretty common when working with sliding harmonics to end up with your finger on a different note from the one you're hearing. This may be a little trippy at first, but you'll get used to it with practice.)

As you slide to wider intervals along the string, you'll notice that you begin to hear more of the closed tone you're fingering than the original harmonic. As your finger moves along the string, the sliding motion tends to mute the harmonic and accentuate the full vibration of the closed string; this is especially true when sliding the higher harmonics. Practice sliding wide intervals and see how far you can slide each harmonic without it becoming obscured by the closed tone.

I can't stress enough that you should use techniques like this carefully. There are many colors and sounds available from the bass—so don't get bogged down in overusing any one technique in the same way. Use your creativity to see how many ways you can apply these ideas to come up with a variety of interesting sounds, all of which can add depth and color to your music.

Michael Manring Ex. 1

harmonics --->

Michael Manring Ex. 2

harmonics --->

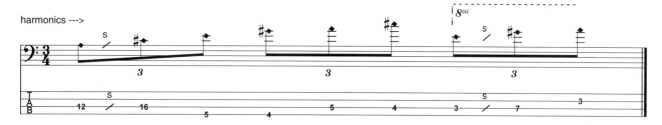

Intonation

I get a lot of questions about intonation. I'm actually pretty happy about that, because in playing any fretless instrument, intonation is THE challenge. As anyone who has even dabbled with a fretless or upright will attest, playing the dang things in tune ain't easy. Not only are they simply physically difficult to play in tune, we're all used to hearing fretted bass, so intonation standards are pretty high. Playing a fretless instrument takes a lot of commitment and it's probably best to accept that there are a lot of things you just won't be able to play on a fretless that you can play on a fretted bass. Nevertheless, there are so many possibilities for nuance on the fretless, so much room for color and expression that in my opinion, the struggle (and even an occasional sour note) is well worth it.

Like so many skills in music, intonation is really about listening. We all have an inborn level of pitch sensitivity and some are gifted (or cursed, depending on how you look at it!) with the almost supernatural ability we refer to as "perfect pitch," but virtually everyone will improve with practice. A good place to start is to train your ear to hear the acoustic phenomenon called "beating" that occurs when two tones of nearly identical pitch are played together. This is an audible modulation or pulsing at the speed of the difference between the notes' frequencies. If the notes are nearly in tune, the beating will be slow, if they're farther apart in pitch the beating will be faster. Beating occurs

because the two sound waves tend to reinforce each other when their peaks align and cancel each other when they are out of phase. Beating is most clearly heard in two simple tones that have the same timbre, and this is why one of the most common methods for tuning a bass is to compare the harmonic at the fifth fret of one string with the harmonic at the seventh fret of the next higher string. For almost everyone, a little beating is actually a pleasant sound and is in fact the basis for effects such as chorus and flange, but when beating gets faster it starts to become more dissonant.

Once you're comfortable hearing beating between unisons it's time to move on to other intervals. Intonation has to do with the relationships between notes, so it's always best to practice intonation with some kind of reference. Your intonation might sound fine when you're playing single-note melodies alone in your room, but when you go to a gig and suddenly have the reference of other musicians to play with it can be a very different story! It's not quite as easy to hear beating in intervals other than unisons, but if you take your time and listen carefully, I think you'll hear that there is a pitch location where each interval sounds most in tune. The pitch reference you use for practicing can be any number of things, but it should be something that is reliably in tune. If you spend all your time practicing to an out-of-tune piano, for instance, you're going to get really good at playing out of tune!

Having a friend who is patient enough to sit and play

scales along with you on a fixed pitch instrument is usually pretty rare, so I'll offer a few suggestions for other options. One of the simplest pitch references is open strings. Just as we used the open G string as a reference for the G at the fifth place of the D string, you can use it as a reference for practically any other note on your E, A, and D strings. Try playing your G string and allow it to ring while you play all the other G's on your bass—the third and fifteenth places on the E string, the tenth and twenty-second place on the A string, and so on. Then play all sorts of G scales on your E, A, and D strings against the open G—major, minor, pentatonic, etc. Do this very slowly and listen for the pitch location for each note in the scale that feels best against the open string. Seconds, sevenths and their compounds are pretty hard to hear, but the rest of the intervals should have a place that really feels like "home." Try the same thing using each of your other open strings as the reference, then try tuning your strings to other notes to give you references for additional keys. The nice thing about using open strings as references is that they are always available, but the drawback is that since one string is always tied up as a reference, you can only work on your intonation on the remaining strings.

This brings us to another indispensable tool for developing your intonation skills: chromatic auto-tuners. Anybody who plays a fretless instrument should have one of these babies. It's hard to believe we ever got by without them! One of my favorite intonation exercises is simply to use a tuner to check every note on my bass, played with every finger. It's slow but effective. I start with my index finger on F at the first fret on the E string, then go up in perfect fourths to B♭ on the A string, the E♭ on the D string, and the A♭ on the G string. Then I check the G♭ at the second place of the E string with my middle finger, the B on the A string, and so on. When I finish checking all sixteen notes in that position (i.e., four fingers on four strings), I move my index finger to the G♭ at the second place of the E string and check all sixteen notes in that position. I continue this to the highest position on the bass. While it does take patience—I find it usually takes me about twenty minutes to a half an hour to complete this exercise—I often feel the benefits for days or even weeks.

One of the most common problems I find that fretless players have is that they learn to play in tune pretty well when they're playing slowly, but as soon as they start to play faster their intonation gets kind of sucky. If you own a sequencer, you can use it to help you work on your intonation for faster lines. Simply set it up to trigger your synth to play scales, lines, melodies or anything else you want to work on (again using a simple, pure sound) and play along. As with beating, it's easiest to hear intonation discrepancies between two notes that have similar timbre, so consider using a bass sound or sample for this exercise. In fact, I actually made samples of my own bass notes for this purpose. If you decide to do this yourself, just make certain that your samples are really in tune!

Because it is easier to hear intonation discrepancies between instruments that sound alike, intonation is more critical in some situations than others. If you're playing a duet with a mandolinist (don't laugh, I've actually been paid for doing this!) you may notice that you can get away with a lot. However, if you're playing harmony lines with another bassist you have to be just about perfect. The most critical situation is if you are multitracking harmony parts to your own melody or bass line in the studio. In this situation there is NO room for error. If even a very short note is out of tune, or if a long note is out of tune for a brief instant, you'll hear it. This is the real acid test for intonation and therefore a superb, albeit frustrating, practice technique. Try playing scales into a recorder, then practice playing along in unison, octaves, and harmony. For the reference part you may want to use a fretted bass that sounds similar to your fretless so that you know you're starting with a reliable source; but then again, in the real world you're likely to find yourself in situations where you need to play along with a part that's not perfect intonation-wise, so consider doing all-fretless multitrack exercises sometimes as well. After you have harmonized scales, move on to working with melodies; almost any melody will do.

Once again, I'd like to stress that you need to take your time with all of these exercises. It's probably best not to try to do them all in one day but to concentrate on one at a time. Developing good intonation is a lifelong process.

ESSENTIAL DISCOGRAPHY

Solo albums: *Soliloquy*, MM; *The Book of Flame*, Alchemy; *Thonk*, High Street; On Windham Hill: *Drastic Measures*; *Toward the Center of the Night*; *Unusual Weather*. **With Michael Hedges** (both on Windham Hill): Aerial Boundaries; Breakfast in the Field. **With Attention Deficit:** The Idiot King, Magna Carta. **With Sadhappy:** *Good Day Bad Dream*, Periscope. **With William Ackerman:** *Imaginary Roads*, Windham Hill. **With Patty Larkin:** *Tango*, High Street. **With Henry Kaiser and Wadada Leo Smith:** *Yo, Miles!*, Shanachie.

MARCUS MILLER

The infamous fretted funk of Marcus Miller (born June 14, 1959, in Brooklyn, New York) has been covered from every angle in Bass Player, *but in a 1994 guest column, Marcus shared insight on his badass fretless playing and melodic phrasing.*

Playing a Melody

Whassup! When it was suggested I do a guest column about the fretless bass melody on "The Sun Don't Lie" (the title track from my third solo album), one thought jumped to mind: the first thing anyone interested in playing a melody should do is learn it with their ears. I feel that way about most things in music, which is why I haven't done any instructional videos or method books. Developing your ear is the most important aspect of being a musician, because it enables you to connect directly to the music on a pure emotional level. Everyone should know how to read, but if you like something learn *all* of it, both by ear and on the page.

Now a little background on the piece itself: The inspiration came from a melody that's been in my head for a long time, so long that I didn't even identify it. I thought it was someone else's song. Those are the best songs, I think—the ones that seem as if they've been written already and you're just discovering them. As I sat down to get it on paper, the melody and the harmony came at the same time, for the most part. The harmony is pretty basic, with various extensions (as in bars 7–9 and 19–20) and substitutions (bars 10–11 are just a play on a II–V–I turnaround) added for color. The twenty bars shown here occur at the top of the track. I used my Sadowsky fretless, recorded direct, and played the melody mostly on the D and G strings up around the twelfth fret. I added a few bass notes on a Fender Rhodes piano during the first nine bars and then played roots on a bass synth, well down in the mix, beginning at bar 11.

When performing the melody on bass, I tried to emulate the way a great singer sings. Jaco was known for being into Frank Sinatra; in this case, I was thinking along the lines of Stevie Wonder. Trying to play like an R&B singer will provide you with all sorts of ways to embellish a note. All the hammer-ons, grace notes, and vibrato markings you see, plus the way I altered the melody the second time through, come from listening to vocalists. For example, when playing the long notes in bars 1, 3, 5, and 13, it sounds silly if you apply the vibrato right off. But if you hit the note and establish the pitch first and then add vibrato, as a singer would, you'll get a much more "natural" sound.

Two points of advice as you approach the music: First, taping yourself and listening back is not only excellent for checking your intonation on fretless, it's essential with any bass. Eventually, you'll hear recurring ideas you dig in your own playing, and you'll be taking the first step toward finding your own style. (Trane used to say, "Tape yourself all the time.") Second, as I said at the top, *learn this piece by ear first.* Then take a look at the transcription and see how it compares to what you heard. Good luck . . . peace.

ESSENTIAL FRETLESS DISCOGRAPHY

Solo Albums: *Marcus*, Concord; *Silver Rain*, Koch; *M2*, 3 Deuces; *Live & More*, GRP; *Tales*, PRA; *The Sun Don't Lie*, PRA; *Suddenly*, Warner Bros. **With Lenny White:** *Streamline*, Elektra. **With Urszula Dudziak:** *Future Talk*, Inner City.

Marcus Miller Ex. 1

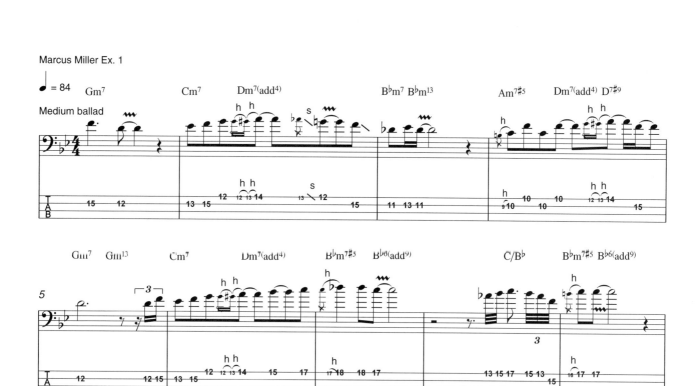

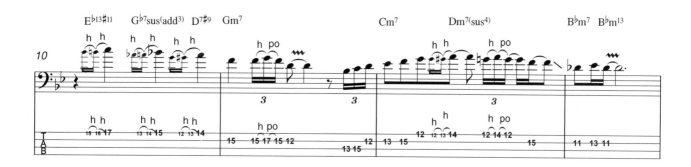

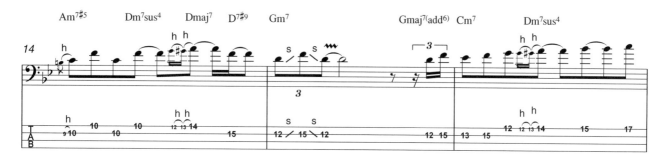

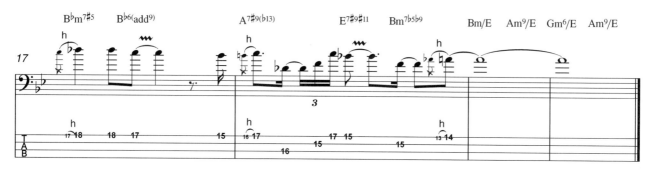

Appendix I: Repair and Maintenance

Through the years, *Bass Player* regularly addressed the repair and maintenance needs of the fretless crowd, through both outside experts and technical columnists.

ASK THE EXPERTS

What do you recommend for the care and maintenance of fretless fingerboards?

Mike Pedulla: Our unfinished fingerboards are given an oil and urethane coating. Each time you change the strings, you should wipe the board with a rag or 3M pad and apply a coat of an oil-urethane mixture. Using a sponge, swirl the mixture around and wipe the fingerboard fairly dry, then let it sit for at least an hour. This helps the wood to retain its stability against seasonal extremes in humidity. It will also help to harden and protect the board against string wear and subsequent levelings, which remove wood and reduce neck thickness. We also recommend nickel-wound roundwound strings, which are easier on the board than steel roundwounds. The polyester-coated necks on our Buzz Basses can pretty much be left alone; the finish will scratch, but that doesn't affect playability. After three or four years of heavy use, the finish may wear through to the board; when that happens, we simply scrape it off and recoat it.

Kevin Kaufman: We offer unfinished fingerboards as a matter of personal preference; we don't like the way an oil-finished board feels. We do, however, recommend using lemon oil for cleaning, because it evaporates quickly. Roundwounds will wear into the fingerboard fairly rapidly; when that occurs, the board should be dressed by a repairman—dressing is the process of leveling the playing surface by planing or sanding. To slow down wear, you can have epoxy, urethane, or polyester resin applied to the fingerboard. It will require little maintenance, and if the coating is thick enough, the fingerboard can be dressed just like wood. Coated fingerboards are prone to chipping on the edges, though, and their density and resilience affect the tone pretty drastically. We use a softer finish than most bass manufacturers, because we've found it provides a warmer tone.

Roger Sadowsky: On an unfinished fingerboard with excessive string wear, we fill in deep grooves with cyanoacrylate glue before sanding—that way, we don't have to remove so much wood—and then resurface the entire board. On a finished board, we wet sand to remove string grooves and then buff. Whether you have a finished or unfinished fingerboard, the most important factor is the kind of strings you use: the coarser the string, the more it will wear the board. Using flatwound or halfround strings instead of roundwounds will slow fingerboard wear, but you should use the strings that give you the right sound—even if it means more visits to your repairman. It's also essential to wipe your strings after playing, especially the undersides where the abrasive crud builds up.

Mike Pedulla *operates M.V. Pedulla Guitars in Rockland, Massachusetts; his fretless Buzz Basses are favored by many top players, including Mark Egan.*

Kevin Kaufman *was Jaco Pastorius's bass technician. Today, he and his partner Tim Daenzer build and repair basses at Kaufman/Daenzer Instruments in West Palm Beach, Florida.*

Roger Sadowsky *runs New York's Sadowsky Guitars. www.sadowsky.com*

BASS TECH
by Rick Turner

Converting a Fretted Bass

When converting a bass from fretted to fretless, you must remove the frets carefully so fingerboard chips don't come out with them. Sure, Jaco may have just pulled 'em out with his teeth and rubbed Silly Putty in the slots (just kidding!)—but with all due respect, you should be a little more careful than he was. Uneven spots on the fingerboard will cause some notes to buzz, but most people want a fretless to buzz evenly on all notes.

I remove frets by self-heating them: running a controlled electric current through the frets with flush-ground end nippers (available from Stewart-MacDonald; www.stewmac.com) so they heat up and slide out easily. You can heat the frets with a soldering iron—but my system is more controllable and relatively gentle, and it puts the heat right where you want it. I use an American Beauty resistance soldering unit with a tweezer handpiece, which I've modified to open wider than normal. The tweezer tongs act as electrodes, which I touch to each end of the fret; the variable-current power supply has a footswitch to turn on the juice. When I zap the fret, the current causes it to heat up to just the right temperature to melt any glue in the slot—as well as to slightly plasticize the wood—allowing clean fret removal. Ebony boards are more subject to "chip-out" than rosewood or maple—but for woody tone and long life, ebony is best.

Installing Fret Lines

Although some people use maple veneer for inlaid lines, I prefer .020" styrene, available through plastics suppliers or hobby shops. Fret slots are generally .022"–.025" wide, so the styrene markers slip in with just the right clearance for glue. To install them, cut strips 1/8" longer than the fingerboard width and a bit wider than the slots' depth; put them in the slots, and then apply superglue (cyanoacrylate or Krazy Glue) to each side of the protruding plastic. The glue will wick easily into all cracks and narrow spaces. After waiting ten or fifteen minutes, apply a second coat. Once the glue has set, file and sand down the excess styrene.

Be very careful with superglue! Don't let it get on the neck finish; if it does, immediately wipe it off. Cyanoacrylate loves to bond to nitrocellulose lacquer. If it gets onto a polyester finish, you can generally remove it with superglue debonder. I got superglue in my eye once, so I have researched its toxicity. It hurt like hell, but the good news is it does no permanent damage, and it's not particularly toxic.

Fingerboard Finishes

Finish options range from the traditional unfinished to super-hard modern polymers. Considerations here are durability and feel; many players prefer a compromise between the two. Most upright players don't use anything except perhaps a little mineral or lemon oil to keep the fingerboard from drying out excessively. Plain ebony is quite hard, polishes great with 600-grit sandpaper, and feels good; also, strings vibrating against bare wood have a nice tone. However, upright bassists don't usually use round-wound strings, which can eat up fingerboards—especially if you have a heavy touch or use a lot of vibrato. Some of my fretless clients can go a couple of years between fingerboard redress jobs, while others need their boards worked on every couple of months.

There are other fingerboard treatments that preserve much of bare wood's tone and feel: tung oil, and one of the modern formulations that contain such resins as polyurethane. Tung oil soaks into the wood and hardens in the pores, making the top .010" to .020" of the wood harder and tougher. You still feel bare wood, but its modified surface can take more abuse. It's easy to keep up, too, as the oils can be reapplied at any time. I've used Formby's products with good results; read and follow the directions (something that took me years to learn).

Hard coatings such as polyester resins and superglue are also sometimes used. Polyester provides a beautiful, glassy fingerboard finish; it's quite wear-resistant and gives a very bright tone. If you use polyester, be sure to get a surfacing formulation, not a casting or laminating resin. The surfacing resins have an additive that skins over the surface, enhancing a good, hard cure. The coating can be sanded and rubbed out to an extremely high-gloss finish. I have also used superglue, built up in thin coats, sanded, and polished. It's particularly good for building up worn fingerboard areas, with or without wood dust mixed in. It works wonderfully, but it's a real pain to apply.

On an instrument of my own, I would lean toward an oil with polyurethane resin as the best of both worlds, but that doesn't mean it's gospel.

Fingerboard Care and Feeding

Fretless fingerboards require more maintenance than fretted ones, especially if you use roundwounds—so if you're not willing to learn how to sand and dress your board, be prepared to have a good relationship with a luthier. Think of this the way race-car drivers do: If you want high performance, be prepared for constant maintenance.

When a fingerboard develops playing-surface wear, buzzes show up just flat of the notes you tend to play the most. The temporary solution is to raise the action, but a better solution is to resurface the board. There seems to be a lot of concern about resurfacing and wearing out a fingerboard—but if you do wear it out, so what? Just put on a new one.

I've come to prefer Birchwood Casey's Tru-Oil sealer and oil for treating fretless boards. It penetrates the wood's surface, dries very tough, and looks good. It won't eliminate wear, but it's not as problematic as superglue. You can get Tru-Oil from Luthiers Mercantile (800-477-4437) or from a gun shop—it's a preferred finish for gun stocks. My father, who hunted ducks from a boat in the Atlantic Ocean, used Tru-Oil to polish the stocks of his favorite shotguns. If Tru-Oil can hold up under those conditions, it's good enough for electric basses!

Intonation Concerns

With an unlined fretless board, theoretically you don't need to set intonation—after all, you should be playing by ear, not by eye. Players of violin-family instruments don't worry about intonating their bridges; they rely on ear training. The same should be true with fretless electric basses. Remember: Intonation, just like tone, is mostly in your fingers. However, you may find with double stops and chords that your fingers just don't want to squish together to make the notes play in tune. If that's the case, experiment with intonating the strings to make your style more in tune.

With a lined fingerboard, the theoretical note position is right on the line, so you'll have to finger right up to it to play in tune. Intonation is affected by the width of your finger pad as well as the action height, so some form of intonation compensation is legitimate. However, it can't be done by the hard-and-fast rules used for fretted basses. You have to decide what your intonation reference is going to be and then intonate your bass to that point. If you're consistently playing flat, move the saddles toward the peghead; if you're playing sharp, move the saddles back toward the instrument's butt end.

Rick Turner has designed and built instruments for several leading manufacturers and now operates Rick Turner Guitars in Southern California.

BASS TECH
by Dan Erlewine

Defretting Made Easy

Recently I helped my friend Larry convert a replacement P-Bass neck from fretted to fretless. I made it look so easy, Larry was sure he could have done the job himself. I agreed with him. All the job entailed was: (1) removing the frets, (2) widening the fret slots to accept black plastic binding strips, (3) installing the plastic strips, (4) applying instant glue to hold the strips in place, and (5) leveling the plastic strips to make them even with the original fingerboard surface.

This is a great D.I.Y. job that doesn't require fancy tools—it's a doable, affordable project. Plus, I'd bet money that any tools you buy for this will get used often, because you'll be hooked on doing your own work.

Fig. 1. I clamped the heel (body end) of the neck to my workbench, using wood blocks to raise it up several inches above the bench's surface. Then I clamped the nut end of the neck to pull the neck back into a gentle, but exaggerated, back-bow. The back-bow opens the fret slots slightly, making it easier to pull out the frets without chipping the wood. Inexpensive bar clamps, available for about $7 apiece, will work fine.

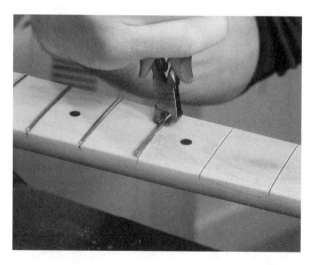

Fig. 2. I removed the frets with a Stewart-MacDonald fret puller. These small, custom-ground, flush-cutting end nippers have narrow jaws that make it easy to pinch under a fret's crown to raise it up and out of its slot. Following the curved fingerboard radius, I "walked" each fret out of its slot. I kept a soldering iron, a cup of water, and cotton swabs nearby in case I needed to heat and moisten the frets so they'd pull out easily. As it turned out, I didn't need any heat, water, or other help.

Fig. 3. A feeler gauge (available at automotive stores) showed that the slots were .024" wide—fairly tight. The plastic binding strips I wanted to use measured .040" thick, so I needed to widen the slots.

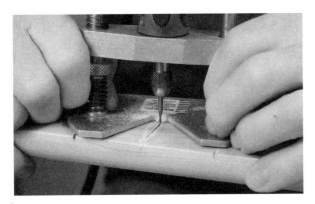

Fig. 4. I used a Dremel Moto Tool with a .031"-diameter cutting bit. Wood typically cuts considerably wider than the actual size of the Dremel bit; additionally, these small routers can be a bit sloppy. I knew that if I used this bit, the slot would end up close enough to .040" that I could tap the plastic binding in with a small hammer. If you don't have a Dremel tool and router base, you could use a fine-tooth hacksaw blade to widen the slots, but practice on scrap first.

Fig. 5. I scraped one flat side of the binding to thin it by .01" or .02". You can use any piece of thin steel with a sharp edge, such as a razor blade, to scrape.

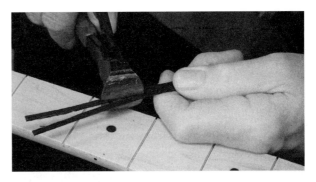

Fig. 6. Each binding strip was 1/4" wide, enough to provide two strips when cut in half lengthwise. I used my flush-cutting fret nippers for the job, although several passes with a sharp utility knife would also work.

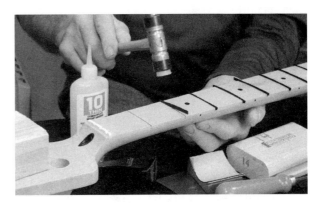

Fig. 7. I cut the halved strips to length, leaving some overhang on each end of the slot to be filed away later. I tapped them in with a small hammer, tapping down one end first, then continuing on across the fingerboard. This way, each plastic strip easily bent to conform to the 14" fingerboard radius as I hammered it tight into its slot. The nippers gave the plastic strips one straight edge and one rough edge. I inserted the frets with the straight edge facing down and tapped them until they bottomed out in the slots, filling the space entirely; this left the rough edges sticking (temporarily) above the fingerboard surface.

Fig. 8. After installing the strips, I ran No. 10 (water-thin) superglue along each side of them. The glue's incredible capillary action takes it deep into the slots, and it sets in less than a minute.

Fig. 9. To remove the bulk of the plastic above the fingerboard surface, I used an 8"-long, 14"-radius wooden sanding block faced with self-sticking 80-grit sandpaper. For a smooth feel, I followed with 120-, 220- and 320-grit papers until the plastic was flush with the fingerboard surface. A radius block is not necessary; a flat sanding block of scrap wood would also get the job done.

Fig. 10. With the trussrod adjusting nut just snug (i.e., barely applying tension to the neck), I checked the fingerboard surface using a long straightedge. The playing surface was perfectly straight from end to end and had retained an even 14" radius from side to side.

The cost of the tools I used in this job (other than common, around-the-house tools) totaled $230.92. Deduct the Dremel router tools if you use a hacksaw blade, and the tool cost is just $66.58. That's a good price, considering you'd probably have to pay an experienced technician between $250 and $350 to do this job—and you get to keep the tools!

Woodshed

You may wonder how to intonate your fretless bass, or if it's even necessary. While the ear lets you adjust constantly, there's certainly some wisdom to having the harmonics in tune before you start. Here are tips from Carl Pedigo, chief luthier for Chicago's Lakland Basses:

"On a lined fretless, I use my fingernail on the line to get the intonation right. Without lines, I use a flexible ruler to make a mark in the middle at the nut and one in the middle at the heel of the neck, and then I use a straightedge to determine the center line. Next, I use a T-square to find a line that's perpendicular to the centerline at the 12th-fret position. On a 35"-scale bass, you do it at 172", but I usually go 3/32" sharp to compensate for your finger pad. I either draw a line there or use a piece of tape to mark it, and intonate from that spot."

ASK BP
by Jonathan Hererra

How does a fretless bass's setup differ from a fretted bass?

The fretless bass has two qualities that make setting it up different from a fretted bass: the missing frets and the *mwah* factor. Most fretted-bass setups strike a balance between easy playability and fret-buzz, but fret-buzz is moot on a fretless. The result is that the strings can be lower overall than on a fretted bass. While the same general rules apply on fretless with regard to trussroad adjustment and string height (more on that in a sec), nut-slot height is an important, oft-ignored factor. Many fretlesses, especially less expensive models that mimic a fretted counterpart, have fretted-bass nut slots. Without frets, a fretless bass's nut slots can go deeper, often by as much as 0.02" per string. Note that a single slot depth across the nut is unacceptable, as the increasing string diameters require slightly different parameters.

Getting back to the relief/string-height balance, fretless players often set up their instruments to actually enhance fingerboard buzz. The buzz is a main ingredient to that desirable *mwah* sound. Experimentation is key here, but an important consideration is that relative to a fretted bass, fretless basses require less relief (amount of the neck's front- or back-bow as determined by the trussrod), particularly if you're aiming for a growling *mwah* tone. Provided the nut slots are well cut, a properly dialed-in fretless neck may be nearly perfectly straight.

Appendix II: Fretting about the Fretless: Observations and Anecdotes from the Pros

Over the years, many of the top bassists interviewed in Bass Player weren't able to get in-depth about their fretless playing, usually because it was an instrument they only doubled on. Nevertheless, many did get to touch on the topic briefly, providing interesting insight.

Alphonso Johnson
(Weather Report, Santana)

"I began playing fretless in 1971. I asked the manager of a club band I was in for an advance so I could buy my first really good bass, and when I was shopping I came across a fretless Fender Precision that blew me away. It was a new concept: an electric neck without frets or fret lines. I figured since I already played upright I would have some affinity for it, but the main reason I bought it was because no one else I knew of was playing one—sort of the novelty of it. Because the club-band gigs involved a lot of reading, I had to woodshed around the clock to get my intonation together without looking at the neck. The key is to know where the notes are on the fingerboard, and then to use that in conjunction with your ears."

Tony Levin
(Peter Gabriel, Session Superstar)

"Fretless—it's a beast. With fretted basses you know what you're going to get, but my fretlesses have all been affected by …I don't know what, the weather, humidity, certainly less margin with string height … so one day it's my lover, and the next gig it's my enemy. Then there's the Jaco factor. He came along and played the way I had only dreamed of playing fretless—but more in tune than even my dreams were! I just put it away for years, not wanting to hear myself trying to measure up to that standard. Eventually I crept out and meekly fashioned a few melodies—still trying. Something that has helped me a lot is to play a five-string (MusicMan) with high C. I don't love the sound of the G string way up high, but this way I can stay in the range where the strings sound best to me. Oh, on "Sledgehammer," I went a different route: I'd never felt much power down low from the fretless, but with an octaver and lots of compression, I hit on a way to get a roar out of that beast!"

Marcus Miller
(Solo Artist)

"As far as the fretless goes, it's important to stick with one instrument and find where the pressure points on your fingers are in relation to the notes on the neck. Beyond that, you just have to keep putting in time, really using your ears. I'll check myself with open strings, but it's always a battle—especially when you play with other instruments that use tempered tunings, like keyboards. You have to look at it like a voice: Voices aren't always in tune. But the main stops—the main resting points—really have to be there. You can use vibrato, but it shouldn't be to cover up bad intonation. It should enhance your playing."

Christian McBride
(Solo Artist)

"The fretless bass is harder to play in tune than the upright. For one thing, there are no landmarks with regard to the shape of the neck or the body as there are on the upright. I purposely didn't get fret lines on my bass, so I could really focus on getting my intonation together. I remember for the first couple of months I was ready to take it back; I just couldn't seem to get it together. I was cool in the lower positions—but once I got further up the neck, look out! As for style, Jaco gave the instrument such an identity, and I wanted to come out of that tradition—the same way the upright has a traditional sound I try to achieve. Beyond that, hopefully something original and musical comes out when I pick up the fretless."

Michael Manring
(Solo Artist)

"Fretless bass is so difficult to play in tune. It's always a challenge, and of course changes in the weather also affect the shape of your fingerboard. Some notes' locations move slightly, and when you get into alternate tunings, the tension also affects a note's placement. So if the string is lower, you have to play the note sharper to keep it in tune. And if it's tuned higher, you have to play a note flatter, because you've got the extra tension of pushing the string down. It's madness, but I just have a feeling about the fretless—the mysterious things about it, the little subtleties that happen when your finger is so close to the string. That keeps me on fretless, even with all the pain of dealing with intonation problems."

Steve Bailey
(Bass Extremes, Solo Artist)

"If a fretless bassist played in tune one hundred percent of the time it wouldn't sound like a fretless bass. Really being able to control one's intonation is the key—not keeping it perfectly in tune, but controlling the out-to-in factor without going completely off the rails. For me, playing in tune is a combination of muscle memory and really fast ear reflexes. It's instantaneous almost; hearing a note that's off and sending the information to my fingers to modify it."

Fernando Saunders
(Lou Reed)

"I've been singing since I was a kid, but having built a career as a sideman, I've rarely been asked to contribute lead vocals. Instead, I compensated by singing through my instrument—that's how I developed my style on fretless bass. As for playing with good intonation, it's all in the ears. Even if you have fret lines, you can't rely on them, because they're not always accurate."

Jeff Ament
(Pearl Jam)

"When we rehearse I play fretless for more than half the songs—not necessarily for the tone or anything but just to work on my intonation. It makes playing more interesting, too. Live it's tougher, but I still play fretless on five or six songs per show. It's the most exciting and fun of all the instruments I have; there's something about the way it sustains and resonates and the things you can do with the notes. There's also something more human and vocal about it. When I just want to try playing something at home, I usually pick up the fretless. The only limitation is for some reason it's not as good for up-tempo numbers. The precision and more staccato nature of the fretted bass is better suited for faster songs. But for things with sustained notes, the fretless works a lot better."

Matt Malley
(Counting Crows)

"Most of the time I prefer to play fretless. You can wring more out of it than you can a fretted bass. But you need to crank up the mids a little when you're playing in a band situation, because you need them for intonation. If it's all bottom and high end, you can't really hear the pitch."

Mark Browne
(Melissa Etheridge)

"Playing rock on fretless was an easier transition than I would have thought. I can play a very foundational role, and then I can move out of that into more melodic material. Playing fretless gives me a chance to explore and exploit nuance and inflection. That's made me a better bass player overall: I listen a lot more, I'm more aware of touch and choice of register, and I take chances I otherwise might not have thought of on a fretted instrument."

John Giblin
(Kate Bush)

"The fretless is almost in danger of becoming extinct, because everyone is still trying to sound like Jaco. I wish people would get just as egotistical because they can play like James Jamerson or Ron Carter."

Select Bibliography

Bacon, Tony, and Barry Moorhouse. *The Bass Book*. San Francisco: GPI Books, 1995.

Coryat, Karl. *The Bass Player Book*. San Francisco: Backbeat Books, 1999.

Jisi, Chris. *Brave New Bass*. San Francisco: Backbeat Books, 2003.

Milkowski, Bill. *Jaco: The Extraordinary and Tragic Life of Jaco Pastorius*. San Francisco: Backbeat Books, 2005.

Mulhern, Tom. *Bass Heroes*, San Francisco: GPI Books, 1993.

_____. "The Singing Bass of Mark Egan." *Guitar Player*, January 1989.

Roberts, Jim. *American Basses*. San Francisco: Backbeat Books, 2003.

_____. *How the Fender Bass Changed the World*. San Francisco: Backbeat Books, 2001.

Internet Resources

All Music (allmusic.com)

Marcus Miller (marcusmiller.com)

Jack Bruce (jackbruce.com)

Gary Willis (garywillis.com)

Yellow Jackets Jazz Quartet (yellowjackets.com)

Mark Egan (markegan.com)

Alain Caron (alaincaron.com)

Steve Bailey (stevebaileybass.com)

Michael Manring (manthing.com)

Bakithi Kumalo (bakithikumalo.com)

Bunny Brunel (bunnybrunel.com)

Fretless Bass (fretlessbass.com)

Fender Musical Instruments (fender.com)

Ampeg (ampeg.com)

Acknowledgments

This book, as well as my *Bass Player* and music journalism career, would not have been possible without the generous help, support, and teamwork of the following: Tom Wheeler, Jim Roberts, Richard Johnston, Bill Leigh, Karl Coryat, Greg Olwell, Jonathan Herrera, Brian Fox, Paul Haggard, Patrick Wong, Damien Castaneda, Ed Friedland, and Matt Resnicoff. Further thanks to Dave Lavender, Neal Rosen, Mark Falchook, Tom Bowes, Jack Knight, Jim Vallis, Danette Albetta, Allan Slutsky, Vinnie Fodera, Joey Lauricella, Pino Palladino, Anthony Jackson, Will Lee, Steve Bailey, Tal Wilkenfeld, John Patitucci, Neil Stubenhaus, Rocco Prestia, Oteil Burbridge, Victor Wooten, Marcus Miller, Bibi Green, Stanley Clarke, Oskar Cartaya, Jeff Berlin, Percy Jones, Victor Bailey, Mike Pope, Janek Gwizdala, Matt Garrison, Glenn Franke, Mike Visceglia, Bill Milkowski, Veronica Martell, Mike Mancini, Sam Kawa, Alan Gross, Joe Capozio, all the great fretless players in the book, the faithful readers of *Bass Player*, the Minissale, Walker, and Stephens families, Bud and Connie Jisi, and, of course, my wonderful wife, Joan Walker.

Contributors

Chris Jisi, senior contributing editor of *Bass Player*

Jim Roberts, founding editor and publisher of *Bass Player*

Bill Leigh, *Bass Player*'s editor in chief

Karl Coryat, a former editor and current consulting editor of *Bass Player*

Richard Johnston, a former editor of *Bass Player*

Greg Olwell, *Bass Player*'s managing editor

Jonathan Herrera, *Bass Player*'s senior editor

Brian Fox, *Bass Player*'s associate editor

Ed Friedland, a former *Bass Player* contributing editor

Elton Bradman, a former *Bass Player* assistant editor

Scott Shiraki, a former *Bass Player* technical editor

Tom Mulhern, a former *Guitar Player* editor and *Bass Player* contributor

Greg Isola, a former *Bass Player* managing editor

Scott Malandrone, a former *Bass Player* technical editor

James Rotondi, a former *Guitar Player* editor and *Bass Player* contributor

Rick Turner, a recurring columnist for *Bass Player*

Dan Erlewine, a recurring columnist for *Bass Player*

Bill Milkowski, a freelance contributing editor to *Bass Player* and the author of *Jaco* (Backbeat)

Anil Prasad, a freelance contributing editor to *Bass Player*

Sean Gerety, a freelance contributing editor to *Bass Player*

Peter Murray, a freelance contributing editor to *Bass Player*

Alexis Sklarevski, a freelance contributing editor to *Bass Player*

Vic Garabrini, a freelance contributing editor to *Bass Player*